# IN THE MIDST OF RADICALISM

D1604387

NEW DIRECTIONS IN TEJANO HISTORY

Alberto Rodriguez and Timothy Paul Bowman,
*Series Editors*

# IN THE MIDST OF
# RADICALISM

*Mexican American Moderates
during the Chicano Movement
1960–1978*

GUADALUPE SAN MIGUEL JR.

UNIVERSITY OF OKLAHOMA PRESS ✳ NORMAN

Library of Congress Cataloging-in-Publication Data

Names: San Miguel, Guadalupe, 1950– author.
Title: In the midst of radicalism : Mexican American moderates during the
    Chicano movement, 1960–1978 / Guadalupe San Miguel Jr.
Other titles: New directions in Tejano history ; volume 3.
Description: Norman : University of Oklahoma Press, [2022] | Series: New
    directions in Tejano history ; volume 3 | Includes bibliographical references. |
    Summary: "A narrative history of the moderate wing of Mexican American
    social justice movements in the 1960s and 1970s"—Provided by publisher.
Identifiers: LCCN 2021028956 | ISBN 978-0-8061-7656-7 (paperback ;
    alkaline paper)
Subjects: LCSH: Mexican American political activists—History—20th century. |
    Chicano movement—History—20th century. | Moderation—Political
    aspects—United States. | Radicalism—United States. | Mexican Americans—
    Civil rights—History—20th century.
Classification: LCC E184.M5 S253 2022 | DDC 305.868/72073—dc23
LC record available at https://lccn.loc.gov/2021028956

*In the Midst of Radicalism: Mexican American Moderates during the Chicano Movement, 1960–1978* is Volume 3 in the New Directions in Tejano History series.

The paper in this book meets the guidelines for permanence and durability of the Committee on Production Guidelines for Book Longevity of the Council on Library Resources, Inc. ∞

＊✳＊

This book is dedicated to all those courageous men and women who
devoted their lives to making this a better world.

＊✳＊

# Contents

# *Acknowledgments*

I thank all the dedicated archivists and librarians from the many archives I visited over several years for helping me to find the documents I was looking for. In particular, thanks to my good friend and colleague Victoria-María MacDonald for her extremely helpful and useful assistance in retrieving research documents buried deep in the National Archives. Gracias also to my friend and colleague Alberto Rodriguez for encouraging me to submit my manuscript to the University of Oklahoma Press and advocating for its publication. The University of Houston provided me with several small grants to conduct research in various archives located throughout the country.

I extend special thanks to my wife, Lorena, for her tremendous support all these years. If she had not assumed additional family responsibilities while I was away on my many research trips, I could not have pursued my research interests and seen this book to publication. Finally, my research and writing over the past several years would have been much less joyful without my daughter, Aimeé-Anali.

# *Abbreviations*

| | |
|---|---|
| AFL | American Federation of Labor |
| AGIF | American G.I. Forum |
| ANMA | Asociación Nacional México-Americana |
| ASU | Arizona State University |
| ATM | August 29th Movement |
| CASA | Centro de Acción Social Autónoma |
| CCR | Committee on Chicano Rights |
| CDC | community development corporations |
| CIO | Congress of Industrial Organizations |
| COPS | Communities Organized for Public Service |
| COSSA | Committee on Spanish Speaking Affairs |
| CPLC | Chicanos por La Causa |
| CSO | Community Service Organization |
| EEOC | Economic Employment Opportunity Commission |
| EOA | Economic Opportunity Act |
| HEW | Department of Health, Education and Welfare |
| HUD | Department of Housing and Urban Development |
| LACA | Latin American Civic Association |
| LNESC | LULAC National Educational Service Centers |
| LULAC | League of United Latin American Citizens |
| MAEC | Mexican-American Education Council |
| MAES | Mexican American Education Study |
| MALDEF | Mexican American Legal Defense and Education Fund |
| MAPA | Mexican American Political Association |
| MASO | Mexican American Student Organization |
| MAYO | Mexican American Youth Organization |
| MEChA | Movimiento Estudiantil Chicano de Aztlán |
| NEA | National Education Association |
| NEDA | National Economic Development Association |

| NFWA | National Farm Workers Association |
| OCR | Office for Civil Rights |
| PADRES | Padres Asociados para los Derechos Religiosos, Educativos, y Sociales |
| PASSO | Political Association of Spanish-Speaking Organizations |
| SBA | Small Business Administration |
| SVREP | Southwest Voter Registration Education Project |
| SWP | Socialist Workers Party |
| TELACU | East Los Angeles Community Union |
| UFW | United Farm Workers (union) |
| UMAS | United Mexican American Students |
| VRA | Voting Rights Act |
| YSA | Young Socialist Alliance |

# *Introduction*

In the past several decades historians have investigated the complex origins, evolution, and legacy of the radical Chicano Movement. Most of these studies have slighted the important role that moderate liberal activists played during this time in promoting significant social change, instead focusing on the activities and organizations associated with radical leaders of the movement. Many highlight individuals such as Reies López Tijerina, Rodolfo "Corky" Gonzales, and Bert Corona, along with college and high school student groups. They also focus on events such as the Chicano antiwar movement, La Raza Unida Party, the Mexican American Youth Organization (MAYO), and the Brown Berets, or on feminists and their struggles against sexism and for Chicana voices in American society.[1] All these individuals and organizations held diverse views, but they were united in rejecting moderate approaches to social change. Distrustful of mainstream institutions, they embraced militancy; demanded rapid, immediate, and at times substantial change; and resorted to direct action tactics and civil disobedience in their campaigns for equality, social justice, and a non-discriminatory society. Established and long-standing leaders of the Mexican American community, like those involved in the League of United Latin American Citizens (LULAC) and the American G.I. Forum (AGIF), according to these activists, were too accommodating and continued to depend on methods that did not upset those in power.[2]

Few studies of the Chicano Movement during the 1960s and 1970s focus on these moderate liberal activists; that is, those who retained faith in the federal government to help solve their problems, trusted mainstream institutions and political leaders to eliminate discrimination, and rejected the politics of protest. This approach, as the historian

Ignacio García noted, required not only "faith in the established institutions" but also "patience in the face of slow change."[3] Although a few moderate activists turned militant during the mid-1960s, the vast majority remained deferential; continued to work with established leaders to counter discrimination in American life; and did not resort to pickets, protests, marches, or demonstrations. Little is known about these individuals. Who were they and how did they contribute to the struggle for social justice and equality? Were they pawns of political leaders or did they stay true to their community and continue to represent their diverse interests within establishment channels? Finally, what impact did their actions have on the Mexican American community and on the historic struggle for social justice waged since the early 1900s?

The moderate activists of the 1960s and 1970s followed in the footsteps of predecessors involved in fighting for equal rights since the late 1920s. Mario T. García has called these activists members of the "Mexican American Generation." This generation came of age during the Great Depression and World War II and worked tirelessly to combat poverty, racism, and discrimination in American life from at least the 1930s to the 1960s.[4]

Mexican American Generation activists were influenced by several important factors. Among these were the decline in Mexican immigrants due to repatriation policies and the Depression in the 1930s, the growing numbers of Mexican-origin individuals born in the United States over the years, and the influence of American institutions such as New Deal agencies, youth clubs, public schools, the Catholic Church, and the military. These activists were further influenced by war experiences in the 1940s and anti-communist sentiments during the Cold War.[5]

Unlike immigrant activists of the early twentieth century, these individuals considered themselves American citizens and embraced what the historian Anthony Quiroz has called fundamental norms associated with being American.[6] Mexican Americans, for instance, embraced patriotism. Many had served in the military and fought for democracy and freedom in World Wars I and II and the Korean War. As members of the military and veterans of foreign wars, they firmly believed in the U.S. republican form of government; in the ideals of

democracy, freedom, and equality embedded in the U.S. Constitution; and in anti-communism. They likewise accepted whiteness as a
legal strategy for fighting racism rather than as a means of distanc-
ing themselves from the African American struggle for racial justice.[7]
Acceptance of these ideals, however, did not mean that they rejected or
abandoned their cultural heritage. Community activists of this period
were proud of their racial and cultural heritage, of the Spanish language, and of Catholicism.[8]

Mexican American Generation activists also generally believed in
social integration, moderate social change, and use of conventional
tactics for achieving social reform.[9] More specifically, they believed in
the existing social structure but not in the status quo, and sought to
eliminate the barriers limiting the community's social acceptance and
economic mobility in mainstream society. Racism and class discrimination would be eliminated through lobbying, advocacy, voting, litigation,
and other conventional methods of social change, not by protests or
demonstrations.[10]

Guided by their consciousness as American citizens of Mexican
descent, these activists engaged in a protracted struggle to achieve full
citizenship rights. They formed new middle-class and working-class
organizations, mobilized their communities, and initiated a systemic,
persistent national campaign to eliminate barriers to citizenship and
improve the society in which they were living.

The middle-class activists who dominated this movement challenged school segregation, exclusion from public facilities and jury service, and political disfranchisement.[11] Working-class radicals broadened
the general civil rights movement by focusing on concerns such as labor
unionization, deplorable wages and intolerable working conditions, and
the plight of immigrants, especially braceros and the undocumented. A
handful of intellectuals also became important in shaping the identity
of this group. Intellectuals joined with community activists and "forged
a new meaning and definition of what it meant to be an American of
Mexican descent."[12]

The struggle for equality had a checkered record of success.
Although Mexican Americans were unable to remove the deep-seated
structural barriers of racial and class discrimination, they did break

down legal barriers to full citizenship and made important strides in access to better education, to the electoral arena, to jobs, and to mainstream institutions.[13] They also provided many local communities with increased city services, better treatment by government officials, and meaningful neighborhood improvements.

During the years of radicalism Mexican American activists continued to promote an agenda of moderate social change aimed at achieving equality, following the lead of the early twentieth-century Mexican American Generation. In other words, the liberal agenda of moderate social change did not end with the emergence of the Chicano Movement. Rather, it continued and expanded. This book examines the role these moderate liberal activists played during the years of radicalism and focuses on individuals who promoted social and educational equality in American life without resorting to protests, demonstrations, or other forms of direct action.

Of the book's five chapters, two focus on the 1960s, and the other three on the 1970s. Chapter 1 deals with the elevation of politically moderate activism to the national level, the struggles for acceptance and recognition, and the role of the Inter-Agency Committee on Mexican-American Affairs in promoting civil rights, education, and poverty reduction. The Inter-Agency Committee on Mexican-American Affairs was a cabinet-level office in the Johnson administration devoted to addressing the concerns of Mexican Americans. Its establishment indicated to Mexican Americans that mainstream political leaders finally accepted them as equals.

Chapter 2 describes the emergence of radical voices within the Mexican American community during the 1960s, the different mobilization approaches they used, the issues they tackled, and the ways they utilized language and culture in local struggles. These voices, I argue, began to drown out the actions of moderate activists who were promoting national equality and social change.

The third chapter focuses on the formation of the national Chicano Movement during the late 1960s and the 1970s. It emphasizes the many forms of nationalism guiding Chicano Movement activists and reviews the types of struggles they initiated from 1969 to 1978. I argue that the

Chicano Movement was ideologically diverse and revolved around four major concerns: class, race, gender, and culture.

Chapters 4 and 5 describe the multiple activities of moderate Mexican American activists during the height of the Chicano Movement. Chapter 4 provides biographies of some moderate activists in the era of radicalism. I argue that their actions expanded the liberal civil rights movement initiated in the early twentieth century. Their actions also indicated that the moderate civil rights movement did not decline or disappear during the Chicano Movement years. Instead it strengthened and diversified because of the courageous and determined efforts of these individuals, many of whom cooperated with Chicanas/os or leveraged Chicana/o actions to get concessions from political leaders in Washington.

Chapter 5 describes the role of moderate activists in school reform. These fearless individuals filed lawsuits against discrimination in education, advocated for special programs designed to meet the diverse needs of Mexican American schoolchildren, and generally worked within the system to improve the educational opportunities of children who were poor and culturally different.

The text ends with a summary and concluding thoughts on Mexican American moderates during the late 1960s and 1970s. I argue that, without resorting to demonstrations or violent protests, they continued ameliorating the inequities Mexican Americans faced in the United States.

## CHAPTER 1

# Seeking National Recognition
## MODERATE MEXICAN AMERICAN ACTIVISTS IN THE 1960s

Since the early 1900s, moderate Mexican American activists have believed in the power of government to solve their problems and have supported gradual social change. As early as 1914, community leaders turned to the courts for support in eliminating segregation, exclusion from juries, and bans from public accommodations. They also used moral suasion or filed discrimination complaints against local and state authorities to persuade political leaders and mainstream institutions, such as schools and law enforcement agencies, to cease denying them their rights as citizens and human beings.[1]

In the 1960s the struggle for social justice and increased opportunities expanded to the national level through Mexican Americans' participation in electoral and presidential politics. They became increasingly militant in the face of neglect from political leaders, but once they gained recognition and appointments to high office, they abandoned direct action tactics, at least on the national level.

## THE MEXICAN AMERICAN CIVIL RIGHTS MOVEMENT
## REACHES THE NATIONAL LEVEL

In the 1960s, as in years before then, civil rights leaders placed their faith in the liberal agenda, specifically that the U.S. government would intervene on their behalf and improve their status in society. Unlike earlier decades, however, they became active on the national level. In 1960 they established Viva Kennedy clubs throughout the Southwest and Midwest, actively working to get the vote out for Kennedy. Some efforts were more centralized than others, but all remained

independent of the Democratic Party structure. An emotional identification with Kennedy as a friend of the barrio, rather than knowledge
of policies and programs, guided most of these efforts. This campaign
unified various Mexican American and Latina/o groups throughout the
country and nationalized Mexican American political activity. In other
words, this effort brought together Mexican American and Latina/o
groups that had not previously worked together.[2]

Having played a key role in the national election, Viva Kennedy
supporters expected important appointments to the executive or judi-
cial branch of the federal government. They received only minor ones.
George I. Sánchez, for instance, was appointed to the National Advisory
Council for the Peace Corps and to the Committee on New Frontier
Policy in the Americas. Hector P. García was offered a special ambas-
sadorship to the West Indies and served on the U.S. delegation to the
United Nations. In 1961, Raymond L. Telles of El Paso was chosen as
U.S. ambassador to Costa Rica.[3] Failure to consider other Viva Kennedy
leaders for more important federal appointments led to disappointment
and disillusionment.[4]

Viva Kennedy activists were successful in getting the first Mexican
American federal judge appointed, but it was not the candidate most
of them supported. The AGIF initially recommended Judge Ezequiel
Salinas to the federal district bench but the nomination got caught in a
battle between Senator Ralph Yarborough and Vice President Lyndon
Baines Johnson (LBJ), who were bitter enemies.[5] Salinas was considered an LBJ man, so the senator blocked the nomination. Ironically, not
even LBJ supported Salinas. Johnson favored Reynaldo G. Garza, an
associate of his. Although Yarborough, the senior senator from Texas,
controlled state appointments, Johnson got permission from Kennedy
to make the appointment.

Other Mexican Americans, especially those who were not involved
in or were only peripherally involved in Viva Kennedy efforts, also failed
to support Salinas. Generally supporters of LBJ, these activists, such as
the prominent J. T. Canales and other Mexican American politicians
from South Texas, preferred Reynaldo Garza, a Brownsville judge.[6]

In response to LBJ's influence and in opposition to AGIF members, Kennedy appointed Garza.[7] The selection of Garza, who hated

the AGIF, disillusioned LBJ's strongest supporters and angered AGIF founder Hector P. García and other activists. After the selection, García voiced his displeasure with LBJ and wrote privately, in a rare use of Spanish: "estos desgraciados no nos quieren dar ni agua" (These good-for-nothings don't even want to give us water [that is, the slightest thing]). Teodoro Estrada, another forum member also wrote to García that Mexican Americans were "fools" for having trusted Johnson.[8]

The realization of their powerlessness, perceived neglect of their political concerns, and need for greater unity encouraged several former Viva Kennedy activists to call a meeting in Victoria, Texas.[9] Their purpose was to discuss the future of Viva Kennedy clubs and how Mexican Americans could increase their political power. This meeting led to the formation of Mexican Americans for Political Action, led by Bexar County Commissioner Albert A. Peña Jr.

Later, a group of leaders representing the California-based Mexican American Political Association,[10] the Texas Mexican Americans for Political Action, the CSO, and LULAC met in Phoenix, Arizona, in an effort to develop greater political unity within the Latina/o community. Their discussions led to the establishment of a new organization, also called Mexican Americans for Political Action.[11]

The new entity, unlike existing ones, was intended to have a nationwide reach, to be independent of the Democratic Party, and to support Mexican Americans for political office. Arguments over labeling, however, quickly undermined the organization. Some activists believed the use of "Mexican" in the organization's name was offensive. Others thought that it was not inclusive of other Latinas/os. Others still felt that it emphasized ethnicity at the expense of American citizenship.[12]

At its second founding convention the coalition changed its name to the Political Association of Spanish-Speaking Organizations (PASSO). This title was a hard-fought attempt at compromise because Latinas/os in various states had different names for themselves. Those in Colorado called themselves Spanish Americans, New Mexicans were Hispanos, Californians were Mexican Americans, and in Texas and elsewhere, they were Latin Americans or Spanish speakers. At the end of the conference, the California contingent refused to join and maintained its state organization, called the Mexican American Political Association

(MAPA). Arizona activists likewise formed their own organization. Activists in New Mexico and other states joined PASSO but also kept their own local or statewide organizations. Controversy over the name led to the establishment of a weak national organization consisting primarily of chapters in Texas, with a few in other states.[13]

Differences over strategy further weakened PASSO. In 1962, PASSO members in Texas supported candidates for statewide office who failed to win, and thereby the organization alienated those that did win. One example was the race for governor. Three candidates—Ralph Yarborough, John Connally, and Price Daniel—were competing for the Democratic nomination. Although members were divided over which candidate to back, at the statewide convention PASSO decided to support Daniel. He however lost the nomination to Connally, an LBJ ally who was mistrusted by many activists.[14] Prior to the election PASSO members requested to meet with him to discuss some of their specific concerns, but Connally declined, and consequently, PASSO withdrew its support for the general election. When Connally won without the organization's endorsement, PASSO's actions alienated Democratic Party leaders and President Johnson. The outcome also showed that the group had no clout at the state level.

After the election fiasco of 1962, PASSO decided to change its tactics. Unable to significantly influence state politics, they turned to local elections. In 1963, PASSO allied with the American Federation of Labor (AFL) in support of an all–Mexican American slate of five candidates for the city council election in Crystal City. These candidates were all working class, had limited educations, and had never previously been involved in local, state, or national Democratic Party activities. Although they did gain control of the city council, they were unable to govern effectively or to retain their seats. The PASSO candidates were replaced the following election with a more diverse slate and with "safe" Mexican Americans.[15]

Participation in this city election, though initially successful, eventually backfired and led to further divisions within PASSO over the appropriate strategy for gaining political office. Some activists opposed forming alliances with labor organizations, supporting working-class Mexican Americans as officeholders, or alienating the political

establishment such as LBJ and his allies in Crystal City. Others felt
that PASSO had to form alliances with any group that would give them
political clout. This new strategy, then, eventually left PASSO powerless and fragmented.[16]

In the meantime, on the national stage, Mexican Americans continued to argue that they were being discriminated against in the work-
place on the basis of national origin and race. They also complained
that they were being excluded from federal employment. Kennedy and
Democratic Party leaders ignored them.

In 1962, the president established an executive committee to
address job discrimination. Known as the President's Committee on
Equal Employment Opportunity, it focused on investigating racial
discrimination by businesses holding federal contracts and by federal employers themselves. Most of the investigations, however, concerned blacks, and Mexican Americans were overlooked. One way of
correcting this, an internal AGIF memo concluded, was to appoint
a "capable Latino or Latinos" to the committee. After much wran-
gling, Dr. Joaquín González, brother of Texas congressman Henry B.
González, was appointed.[17]

Despite this appointment, the committee continued to investigate
mostly cases involving African Americans. According to one source, only
2 percent of the committee's probes dealt with Mexican Americans.[18]
Mexican American activists charged the committee with neglecting
employment problems faced by Spanish-speaking Americans. LBJ, in
response to this charge, met with several activists and urged them to
submit evidence of discrimination so that the committee could deal
with it. Despite this pledge, Mexican American concerns were still
being neglected, as indicated at the Regional Conference of Community Leaders on Equal Employment Opportunity, convened in November 1963. A few Mexican American activists were invited to participate
in this important conference, but there were no sessions on the special
employment discrimination problems confronting Mexican Americans.[19] Neglect continued to characterize federal policy on discrimination against Mexican-origin people.

The exclusion of Mexican Americans and their concerns from the
discourse on employment discrimination most likely was due to the

nature of race relations in the United States. Most social problems were framed in the context of a dual notion of race: black or white. Mexican Americans, unlike other racially mixed groups, were constructed as white by the courts and federal agencies, even though they did not receive the benefits and privileges of whiteness.[20] Because of Mexican Americans' legal classification as white, the federal government neglected their needs and concerns and concentrated on addressing issues facing African Americans. Mexican American activists began to argue that their community had unique problems not being addressed by the federal government.[21]

In 1963, Kennedy was assassinated and Lyndon Johnson assumed the presidency. After the assassination, Mexican Americans rallied behind LBJ. During the 1964 elections, they again became key players through the Viva Johnson campaign but their role was ignored in the landslide victory. The Viva Johnson campaign was dismantled after the elections.[22]

Many Mexican American leaders, especially Hector García and George Sánchez, believed that President Johnson, who was familiar with their community, would be more responsive to them than Kennedy had been. He, however, also ignored Mexican Americans and their concerns. Governmental neglect of their issues led to further disenchantment and frustration with political leaders during the Johnson administration.

Despite Spanish-speaking Americans' strong support in the election, Johnson failed to make any important Mexican American federal appointments between 1964 and 1966, or to include them in any significant way in the formulation of poverty and civil rights legislation. An example occurred with the drafting of the Economic Opportunity Act (EOA) of 1964. LBJ issued the call for the Great Society in January 1964. When he formed taskforces to develop this legislation, no Mexican Americans were asked to participate on them. Despite their exclusion from the drafting of the bill, the AGIF strongly supported its enactment. As the legislation was making its way through Congress in 1964, AGIF urged its members to support the bill and not drop the ball on this one.[23]

The bill passed and became one of the most important pieces of poverty legislation of the 1960s. Its provisions led to the establishment

of hundreds of poverty programs and to the participation of new sectors
of the Mexican American population in addressing social and political
issues in their neighborhoods. These programs provided young people
and community activists with increased opportunities to form new
organizations under their control dedicated to community improvement and empowerment. It also provided them with employment to
engage in community activism, to recruit and train youth volunteers for
these programs, and to gain useful organizing and administrative experiences. The EOA and the War on Poverty, according to the historian
Marc Simon Rodríguez, along with the United Farm Workers (UFW)
union in California, served as the foundation for Mexican American
activism in the U.S. Southwest and Midwest.[24]

In April 1965, the AGIF protested Mexican Americans' exclusion
from the drafting of federal guidelines for implementing War on Poverty programs in the Southwest.[25] It also complained that relatively few
programs were located in Mexican American communities and that few
Mexican Americans were hired to implement those that did exist. An
AGIF leader from Washington, DC, Rudy Ramos, urged Washington to
take affirmative steps to hire Mexican Americans.[26]

In the fall of 1965, LBJ announced a White House Conference on
Civil Rights to be held in the summer of 1966. Again, Mexican American activists and their concerns were not included in conference planning or invited to the conference itself. In response to their effective
exclusion from the national discourse on civil rights, Rudy Ramos
called for Mexicans Americans to demonstrate and take to the streets.
However, notwithstanding their frustration with the Johnson administration, most activists were not ready for this type of action.

Unable to get any recognition in the first half of the decade, Mexican
American activists at the national level became more militant by 1966
and began to use direct action tactics selectively to demand attention.
Although the majority of these individuals had historically refrained
from engaging in protests, they were inspired to move beyond accom-
modation by the national boycott of table grapes initiated by César
Chávez; the mass rallies, marches, and demonstrations by black civil
rights activists; the growing popular opposition to the war in Vietnam;
and even the riots in black communities. The lessons of protest, in other

words, were not lost on Mexican American liberal activists. After being ignored by Presidents Kennedy and Johnson, they felt that they needed to take more forceful action. LULAC President Alfred Hernández best exemplified this new attitude: "What does it take? What must we do?" he asked rhetorically at one of their meetings. "While I do not condone violence, it may be that we too should resort to marches, sit-ins, and demonstrations." And beginning in 1966, they did become more assertive in their demands for recognition.[27] In January 1966, for instance, MAPA activists from California walked out of a local Economic Employment Opportunity Commission (EEOC) hearing to protest the ignoring of their concerns and the disrespect with which Executive Director Herman Edelsberg treated them and their community. At the meeting Edelsberg blamed Mexican Americans for their own problems and accused them of being "disorganized, distrustful and jealous of other minorities."[28]

Two months later Mexican Americans representing a larger number of community and civic organizations from the Southwest walked out of a national EEOC meeting in Albuquerque, New Mexico, in protest over the absence of Mexican Americans on the commission and the neglect of their particular concerns in federal employment.[29] Representatives of each of the four major organizations at the meeting—LULAC, AGIF, PASSO, and the Latin American Civic Association (LACA)—lodged separate complaints against the EEOC. This walkout, as the political historian Craig A. Kaplowitz noted, reflected their frustration with not only the EEOC but the federal government as a whole. It also showed the new willingness by Mexican Americans to take direct action and to express unity on a particular issue.[30]

After walking out, the leaders convened in another room to draw up resolutions to send to President Johnson. They formed a new group called the Mexican American Ad Hoc Committee on Equal Employment Opportunity and demanded a meeting with the president to address their concerns. They also increased their criticism of the federal government's failure to understand Mexican American problems and threatened to use more aggressive methods if they continued to be ignored. Rudy Ramos immediately filed an employment discrimination complaint with the U.S. Commission on Civil Rights against the EEOC.[31]

The following month another well-known activist named Bert Corona joined Rudy Ramos in drafting a letter to the White House. They warned that Mexican Americans were discontented and defiant, and that they planned on picketing the proposed June White House Conference on Civil Rights to show their displeasure with the federal government's neglect of their concerns.[32] Unbeknown to Corona, Ramos, and others, the president was already planning to meet with a few of these moderate Mexican American leaders. On May 26, 1966, he met at the White House with Alfred Hernández (LULAC), Augustín Flores, Hector P. García (AGIF), Bert Corona (MAPA), Roy Elizondo (PASSO), and Robert Ornelas of the Equal Opportunity Office of the Department of Defense.[33]

These individuals presented three major grievances with the administration. They had been excluded from the White House Conference on Civil Rights to be held the following month, they were being obstructed by the EEOC, and there were no Mexican American White House aides. Johnson refused to appoint a Mexican American aide, arguing that this would lead to separate demands from other groups for their own representatives. He did however agree to hold a White House conference on Mexican American civil rights and to appoint a Mexican American to the EEOC. This promise of a White House conference would become one of the biggest points of contention between the president and Mexican American activists in the months to come. Before the meeting ended, Johnson agreed to provide immediate funding for Operation SER, a Mexican American job-training program.[34] The president's concessions appeased most of the activists but a few still chose to engage in militant actions. In June 1966, Rudy Ramos and a few others picketed the White House Conference on Civil Rights despite opposition to this action from most Mexican American leaders.[35]

Over the next several months, President Johnson, preoccupied with the war in Vietnam and the growing opposition to it by the American public, ignored the promises he had made to Mexican American activists. This reignited the anger of activists, especially Bert Corona, Ernesto Galarza, and Rudy Ramos. They and other leaders throughout the Southwest continued to press the president to fulfill his pledges to appoint a Mexican American to the EEOC and to hold a White House conference on Mexican American civil rights.

Johnson was interested in holding the conference in the spring of 1967, but he wanted the cooperation of governors. Texas Governor John Connally refused to participate because of his strained relations with Mexican Americans. Johnson's aides advised the president that it would look bad if a conference were held without the presence of Texas officials. Toward the latter part of 1966 the White House began to have doubts about the conference and to reassess this decision. In early January 1967, Johnson decided to forgo the conference without informing Mexican American activists of his decision.[36] His aides encouraged him to hold some other type of meeting but outside of Washington, DC. He took their recommendation under consideration but did not make an immediate determination.

Johnson did however move to appoint a Mexican American to the EEOC. On March 13, 1967, he chose Vicente Ximenes. Ximenes, although a member of the AGIF, was well liked and acceptable to all other groups, especially LULAC, who had expected one of their members to be appointed. Mexican American activists appreciated this gesture and felt that this was a step in the right direction.[37] The appointment would temporarily appease their anger.

In June, Johnson held a swearing-in ceremony in Washington for Ximenes. At the event, he surprised everyone present by announcing that he was also appointing Ximenes to be chair of a newly formed agency known as the Inter-Agency Committee on Mexican-American Affairs. This was no ordinary committee. In addition to Ximenes it consisted of five of Johnson's cabinet members: Secretary of Agriculture Orville L. Freeman; Secretary of Labor W. Willard Wirtz; Secretary of Health, Education, and Welfare (HEW) John W. Gardner; Secretary of Housing and Urban Development (HUD) Robert C. Weaver; and Director of the Office of Economic Opportunity Sargent Shriver.[38] The Inter-Agency Committee would have three major charges, Johnson informed the crowd. It would work to increase the presence of Mexican Americans in the federal government, ensure that they received additional federal funds, and create new programs aimed at meeting their diverse needs.[39]

Most Mexican American activists were overjoyed with Ximenes's appointments and with the formation of the Inter-Agency Committee. Ximenes and the AGIF, in particular, interpreted these actions as indicative that they were now insiders and were fully accepted as equal partners in the shaping of federal policies. "We became part of the political mainstream," noted Ximenes years later.[40]

## ORGANIZING THE CABINET COMMITTEE HEARINGS

One of Ximenes's major tasks was to organize what was originally intended to be the White House conference on Mexican American civil rights that Johnson had promised he would hold. By August 1967, given the growing hostility toward the government from Mexican Americans, the president's aides proposed holding a cabinet committee meeting in the Southwest in place of the White House conference.[41] At this hearing Mexican Americans could present their concerns and recommendations directly to the cabinet secretaries participating in the Inter-Agency Committee on Mexican-American Affairs. The cabinet members, in turn, would develop legislative and executive solutions to address this input. President Johnson agreed, instructing Ximenes to organize a hearing in El Paso, Texas, in October.[42] LBJ was planning on signing a treaty with Mexican president Gustavo Díaz Ordaz in that city in October and thought that Mexican Americans would welcome the opportunity to be present.

Ximenes had only a couple of months to organize this hearing and ensure that all the cabinet secretaries on his committee would be present. He immediately went to work, first obtaining a facility for the conference, then ensuring the cabinet members would attend. Finally, in consultation with the president and other officials, he developed a list of possible presenters, mostly moderate community leaders. Not invited were some of the more radical members of the emerging Chicano Movement such as César Chávez, leader of the UFW; Reies López Tijerina, head of the land grant movement in New Mexico; Corky Gonzales, chair of the Crusade for Justice in Colorado; or college and community youth leaders from California and Texas. The failure to invite any of these individuals became a major sticking point for large numbers of Mexican American activists.[43]

In September 1967, Ximenes informed Mexican Americans that the Inter-Agency Committee would hold a hearing on Mexican American concerns in El Paso the following month.[44] The announcement that a hearing instead of a White House conference would be held and that only moderates would be invited to attend and present did not sit well with several Mexican American leaders, especially the more activist ones such as Bert Corona, the labor leader Ernesto Galarza, college students from the Southwest, and Corky Gonzales. Some of them felt betrayed once again by Johnson and his promises. Over the next several weeks, various groups held meetings in California, Texas, and New Mexico to discuss how to respond. Should they attend or boycott the hearings?[45] MAPA, Gonzales, and Tijerina decided to boycott.[46] College students in California and Texas decided to go but only to picket the hearings.[47] Despite having reservations about the purposes of the hearings, both Galarza and Corona elected to attend. Although the MAPA state organization officially resolved to boycott the hearings, Corona later recalled that he and other MAPA members decided to attend in order "to use the El Paso conference as a forum to express our grievances."[48] The vast majority of Mexican American organizations, including AGIF, LULAC, and PASSO, supported the hearings and made plans to be present.

All the cabinet members on the Inter-Agency Committee, President Lyndon Johnson and Vice President Hubert Humphrey, and a few other officials showed up.[49] Also present were many other government officials and some 1,500 to 2,000 representatives of many Mexican American organizations from the Southwest and Midwest, as well as a few from Puerto Rico. The conference hearings were held in several hotels throughout El Paso.[50] Fifty-one individuals testified for twenty minutes apiece on a variety of topics.[51] Some of the speakers were highly critical and "profoundly" skeptical of the government's intentions.[52] Most however were cordial and grateful for the opportunity to have a voice.[53] The majority of individual presenters believed in the goals of the Inter-Agency Committee on Mexican-American Affairs and trusted that the government officials had come "to hear solutions to Mexican American problems, assure that Federal programs were reaching the Mexican Americans . . . , and seek out new programs that may be necessary to handle problems that are unique to the Mexican American community."[54]

The three-day event opened on Friday to pickets by college students. On Saturday, President Johnson showed up with Governor Connally, whom Mexican Americans in Texas despised for his failure to support farmworkers' rights in the state and for violently suppressing a melon strike in 1966. Once Johnson finished speaking, the conference organizers announced that the presentations scheduled for that day were being cancelled so that the attendees could be present for the signing of the Chamizal Treaty between Presidents Johnson and Díaz Ordaz. Many individuals responded to the announcement with jeers and walked out of the conference to join an alternative conference that more radical contingents were holding in the barrios of El Paso. Sunday's speeches proceeded without any further interruptions.

The alternative gathering, dubbed by most as the Raza Unida conference, was planned by several left-wing activists, including Ernesto Galarza and Corky Gonzales. Similar to the Cabinet Committee Hearings, but held in more modest facilities and with significantly more working-class and grassroots organizers, the Raza Unida conference covered topics pertaining to education, the grape boycott, land rights, employment discrimination, and cultural rights, passing a resolution in support of each issue. At the end of this conference, the attendees issued a statement known as "El plan de la Raza Unida," a highly nationalistic and militant document that affirmed the magnificence of La Raza and proclaimed that "the time of subjugation, exploitation, and abuse of human rights of La Raza in the United States is hereby ended forever."[55]

The attendees at the Cabinet Committee Hearings also spoke on a variety of topics, including culture, education, federal employment, appointments to federal positions, and War on Poverty programs. Unlike their counterparts at the Raza Unida conference, participants in the committee hearings presented a variety of concrete solutions to the problems they were facing. Among some of their recommendations were better understanding and consideration of Mexican culture in federal programs, support for bilingual education, appointment to and hiring of Mexican Americans in federal positions, increased community involvement in the implementation of War on Poverty programs, greater funding of these programs, and enhanced cooperation among private industry, government officials, and Mexican Americans.[56]

Both conferences were declared successes by their organizers. Radical activists argued that the Raza Unida conference unified them as a group and laid the basis for the emergence of the Chicano Movement in the Southwest. Moderate activists, on the other hand, argued that the Cabinet Committee Hearings were "an historic event." "Never before," stated Ximenes, the architect of the hearings, "has a President, a Vice President, cabinet members, heads of agencies, and other high government officials gathered outside of Washington in one location to hear the people of a minority group make recommendations regarding their problems."[57] For him and many others, these hearings marked the beginning of significant change for Mexican Americans.

## IMPLEMENTING RECOMMENDATIONS FROM THE CABINET COMMITTEE HEARINGS

Over the next several months, while leftist leaders criticized the administration for neglecting Mexican Americans, marched on behalf of farmworkers' rights, conducted walkouts at public schools, and protested mistreatment in the War on Poverty programs, moderates like Ximenes and members of the AGIF and LULAC quietly and diligently worked with the president and the cabinet secretaries to implement the many "detailed, imaginative, realistic, and above all, constructive" recommendations made at the hearings.[58]

Probably one of the most important steps Johnson took following the hearings was to sign the first bilingual education bill passed by Congress in December 1967.[59] For several years moderate Mexican American activists and educators had been pushing for the enactment of bilingual education legislation that would address the linguistic and academic needs of Mexican American children attending public schools in the Southwest. At the Cabinet Committee Hearings in October, community leaders expressed a great deal of support for the bill, and enacting it was one of the major recommendations in the final report to the Johnson administration.[60] The Bilingual Education Act acknowledged the presence of millions of non-English-speaking children in the nation's public schools for the first time in history and provided federal funds for local school districts willing to develop innovative educational programs to address their linguistic, cultural, and academic needs. The majority of these children were Spanish speakers.

Another major recommendation in the Cabinet Committee report was the appointment of Mexican Americans to all federal agencies within the executive branch. With the support of Ximenes and the cabinet members on his committee, President Johnson created or encouraged the creation of several new federal agencies and committees with specific responsibilities to Mexican Americans and made several appointments to them.[61] (Kaplowitz argues that these were mostly mid-level appointments.) For instance, he established the Mexican American Unit within the Department of Education and the Mexican American Studies Division in the U.S. Commission on Civil Rights. He also appointed two key individuals to head these offices, Dr. Henry M. Ramírez and Dr. Armando M. Rodríguez. Rodríguez served as director of the Mexican American Studies Unit while Ramírez headed the Mexican American Studies Division.

Ramírez, a well-known educator from California, helped design and implement what came to be known as the Mexican American Education Study (MAES), the first nationwide survey of the conditions and practices hindering the education of Mexican-origin children in the United States.[62] Under his leadership, the U.S. Commission on Civil Rights conducted a four-year study of the schooling opportunities for Mexican American children in the Southwest, compiling information on conditions, educational practices, and educational achievement of these children in the schools they attended.[63] The series of reports the U.S. Commission on Civil Rights issued between 1971 and 1974 are as follows:

I. *Ethnic Isolation of Mexican Americans in the Public Schools of the Southwest* (1971)

II. *The Unfinished Education—Educational Practices Affecting Mexican Americans in the Southwest* (1972)

III. *The Excluded Student* (1972)

IV. *Mexican American Education in Texas: A Function of Wealth* (1972)

V. *Teachers and Students—Differences in Teacher Interaction with Mexican American and Anglo Students* (1973)

VI. *Toward Quality Education for Mexican American Children* (1974)

These reports documented what Mexican American activists and scholars had been arguing for years: that discriminatory and rigid educational policies and practices undermined the identity and achievement of Mexican American children in the public schools, specifically,

1. Mexican American public school pupils were significantly isolated by district and by school within a district.
2. Mexican Americans were underrepresented among school professional personnel and on boards of education. Where they were found, it was mostly in predominantly Mexican American schools or districts.
3. The proportion of students who remained in school through the 12th grade was lower for minority than for Anglo students.
4. A disproportionately large number of Mexican American students failed to meet age and grade-level benchmarks for reading skills.
5. The reading achievement gap for minority children became more severe as they advanced in age and grade.
6. Grade repetition rates were higher for Mexican American than for Anglo students.
7. Mexican American students were up to seven times more likely to be overaged than their Anglo counterparts.
8. Mexican American students were underrepresented in extracurricular activities.

These studies contested several dominant interpretations of school success. One of these held that school failure was due to a culture of poverty or the cultural disadvantage of families and children. This interpretation blamed the child or the child's family for low achievement.[64] The MAES reports showed that school practices and conditions, not the children's culture or home lives, limited equal educational opportunities for Mexican American students and contributed to their alienation, hostility, and school failure. These reports provided the basis for many reforms in the public schools during the 1970s and 1980s and constituted the most important findings on the education of Mexican Americans in the country at mid-century.[65]

Meanwhile, Armando Rodríguez, an educator from San Diego, California, became a forceful national advocate for Mexican American education, for Mexican American students who walked out of their public schools to protest discrimination, and for migrant children who had been neglected by the U.S. educational system. On listening tours, he visited with community leaders, parents, and students throughout the country, supporting their efforts to bring about change. Consistently, he argued that although the federal government had the resources to initiate reforms, many of the obstacles children faced in school could be solved only through community involvement.[66]

Rodríguez had a strong supporter in one of his staff members, Guadalupe "Lupe" Anguiano.[67] One of the most active feminists in the emerging Chicano Movement, Anguiano had been involved in social justice and poverty causes for decades. In the mid-1960s, President Johnson charged her with helping to establish the Mexican American Unit in the Department of Education, and once the unit was established, she was hired as a staff member.[68] She and Rodríguez had previously consulted with Texas Senator Ralph Yarborough in drafting the Bilingual Education Act, which both lobbied for once they joined the Department of Education.[69]

In 1968 President Johnson also established the National Advisory Committee on Mexican American Education, charged with advising the commissioner of education regarding issues affecting Mexican American youth and with assisting Rodríguez to accomplish his goals. The majority of the fourteen members of the committee were Mexican American educators and community activists.[70] Although not established until early 1968, the committee published its first report on the educational status

of Mexican American education by the latter part of the year. Titled
*The Mexican American: Quest for Equality,* the report presented shock-
ing statistics demonstrating the pervasive failure of Mexican American
schoolchildren, identified six major issues for improving their education,
and made specific recommendations on how local, state, and national
officials should remedy the problem of school failure.[71]

Finally, President Johnson appointed Hector P. García to the U.S.
Commission on Civil Rights. Dr. García was simultaneously one of
Johnson's most vocal critics and one of his strongest supporters. Once
appointed to the commission, García immediately persuaded the members to hold a hearing on civil rights violations against Mexican Americans in the Southwest.[72] This hearing was held over several days in
December 1968 in San Antonio, Texas, to collect information regarding civil rights issues facing Mexican Americans in education, employment, economic security, and administration of justice. The intent was
to explore in one city, San Antonio, civil rights problems that were
representative of violations found elsewhere in Texas and in Arizona,
California, Colorado, and New Mexico.[73] Several local officials, including Representative Henry B. González from San Antonio, criticized
the secrecy of the hearings.[74] Among the findings were that Mexican
Americans experienced pervasive racial and cultural discrimination in
the schools, courts, and economy. Moreover, most Mexican Americans
were poor, abused by law enforcement agencies, and misunderstood by
Anglo Americans in the Southwest.[75]

President Johnson also sought to implement recommendations from
the October hearings calling for greater hiring of Mexican Americans
within the federal government. Ximenes himself had been working to
increase the hiring of Mexican Americans in all the federal agencies.
One of his major tasks as chair of the Inter-Agency Committee was
to establish a taskforce within each cabinet department, charged with
identifying how various federal agencies could attract Mexican Americans. In early 1968, President Johnson, in honoring these recommendations, instructed all federal agencies to work together to increase
the hiring of Spanish-speaking Americans, to require employees who
served large Spanish-speaking populations to know Spanish, and to
recruit employees of Spanish-speaking backgrounds (that is, Latinas/os).[76]

In addition, he directed the secretary of labor to initiate job-training programs to attack what he called "hard-core rural and urban unemployment." Many of these programs benefited Mexican Americans in the Southwest.[77]

In addition, President Johnson directed HUD to identify a number of southwestern cities for inclusion in Model Cities, a program aimed at improving urban quality of life. Among the cities selected were San Antonio, Eagle Pass, and Waco, Texas; Denver, Colorado; Albuquerque and Trinidad, New Mexico; New York City, and San Juan, Puerto Rico.[78]

Before he left office in December 1968 the president took two additional actions. First, he issued a presidential proclamation establishing Hispanic Heritage Week. At Ximenes's instigation, President Johnson asked Congress to pass a joint resolution allowing him to issue this proclamation, which Congress willingly agreed to do. "Wishing to pay special tribute to the Hispanic tradition," the congressional joint resolution stated, "and having in mind the fact that our five Central American neighbors celebrate their Independence Day on the fifteenth of September and the Republic of Mexico on the sixteenth, the Congress by House Joint Resolution 1299, has requested the President to issue annually a proclamation designating the week including September 15 and 16 as National Hispanic Heritage Week."[79] In order to make this a permanent event, Ximenes persuaded the president to work with Congress to enact legislation establishing Hispanic Heritage Week. A bill to this end was introduced in 1968 but was not passed.[80]

Second, President Johnson ordered that Mexican Americans be counted as a separate category in the 1970 U.S. census. Ximenes and other Mexican Americans advocated that the nation needed more systematic data collection on Mexican Americans and other Spanish-speaking minorities. By May 1969, Census Bureau Director A. Ross Eckler had agreed to add a question regarding the origin or descent of Spanish-speaking individuals in the United States. "As a result," he noted, "we will have a more comprehensive coverage of this group in the population than previously."[81]

The significant increase in national recognition of Mexican Americans was reflected in their appointment to federal positions, the channeling of War on Poverty resources to them, and the growing number of reports showing discrimination based on language, culture, and class. These gains resulted from countless hours of lobbying, persuading, and cajoling by Ximenes, Rodríguez, Ramírez, Anguiano, and many others within and outside of the federal bureaucracy. Notwithstanding the neglect of their concerns during the first half of the 1960s, moderate Mexican American leaders maintained hope that mainstream political leaders and the federal government in general would not abandon them. They continued to place their faith in these leaders and the federal government to solve the problems confronting their community. In other words, they continued to believe in the moderate agenda of gradual reform even as a growing chorus of radical voices emerged during the second half of the 1960s. The leftist presence undoubtedly benefited the moderates fighting for national recognition and resources, given that the Johnson administration had to choose to negotiate with one wing or the other. But who were these radicals and what influence did they have on the moderates over time? Would radicalism drown out or supplement moderate voices in the community? Would radicalism undermine or strengthen the liberal agenda of social reform? The following chapter focuses on the emerging radical voices in the Mexican American community and issues on which they differed from moderate ones.

## CHAPTER 2

# Radical Voices Emerge in the 1960s
## MODERATES TAKE A BACK SEAT

As moderate Mexican Americans were seeking recognition from the president, leftist voices were emerging in the Southwest. These radical activists did not accept the premise that, over time, the federal government would respond to the community's problems. They were not interested in government positions or in lobbying for the passage of specific legislation. Unlike moderate leaders at the national level, they sought to empower local communities that were poor, disenfranchised, and voiceless to solve their own problems.

Their objective was to organize various groups to fight for Mexican Americans' rights in the fields, rural areas, cities, institutions, and organizations. Although tolerant of lobbying, negotiation, and litigation, the new radicals contested the status quo and embraced mass mobilization, marches, demonstrations, and boycotts as legitimate means of struggle. Unlike established Mexican American activists, most of them also heartily embraced the Spanish language and Mexican culture as tools of mobilization. Some were highly critical of mainstream political leaders, institutions, and ideals, and especially of the concept of assimilation. These activists rejected aspects of the moderates' liberal agenda and used less conventional methods to bring about change. They also introduced new issues, such as labor rights, land loss, urban reform, feminism, and identity construction.

Radicalism was nothing new in Mexican American history. Since the mid-1800s a radical tradition had existed in the community, but it was crushed in the late 1950s by powerful anti-communist and anti-immigrant forces. In the mid-1960s the left wing re-emerged and promoted cultural nationalism, feminism, and militancy, setting the stage for Chicano Movement activists in the late 1960s and early 1970s. Among the most important voices that emerged in the 1960s were those of César Chávez and Dolores Huerta in California, Reies López Tijerina in New Mexico, Corky Gonzales in Colorado, Francisca Flores in California, and youth leaders in several southwestern states.

## THE RADICAL TRADITION IN MEXICAN AMERICAN HISTORY

Although most Mexican Americans historically have used accepted means to struggle against racism and discrimination in American life, since the nineteenth century a vibrant tradition of radical activism has been present in the community.[1] By "radical" I refer to Mexican American leaders who (1) held ideas that dominant leaders in U.S. society or the Mexican American community viewed as un-American, foreign, or non-mainstream; (2) used militant and aggressive language in seeking social justice; and (3) questioned or rejected legalistic means such as litigation, legislation, or lobbying to achieve their ends and instead utilized armed struggle, violence, and direct-action tactics.

The roots of this radical tradition can be found in the Mexican-origin community's violent responses to racism and discrimination in the second half of the 1800s. Individuals like Joaquín Murrieta, Tiburcio Vásquez, and Juan Cortina responded to defamation, bodily assault, and mistreatment by engaging in violence against Anglos. Historians have referred to such individuals as social bandits.[2] A few local communities engaged in violent collective action in response to the appropriation of their rights, property, and resources. A good example was Las Gorras Blancas (the White Caps) in New Mexico. In 1890, responding to unfair railroad fares and the use of barbed wire to fence off land that had formerly belonged to them, the group engaged in raids, intimidation, and destruction of property. More particularly, they burned barns and haystacks, cut barbed wire fences, and sabotaged railroad lines. They also used militant language against the Anglo settlers and corrupt politicians who exploited the Mexican-origin population and robbed them of their lands.[3]

In the early decades of the twentieth century the radical tradition assumed new forms, generally abandoning violent tactics in favor of nonviolent direct action but also becoming more militant. A few radicals did however continue to use violence in defense of their rights or in opposition to Anglo authority. Two examples are the cases of Gregorio Cortez, who shot an Anglo sheriff in self-defense in 1901, and of the participants in the 1915 Plan de San Diego revolt. Yet historians have also noted that the Plan de San Diego marked the end of armed action against Anglo injustice and the shift to other methods of struggle.[4]

Examples of militancy and direct action can be seen in the support Mexican-origin individuals gave to the anarchist Ricardo Flores Magón, in their acceptance of socialist ideas and leaders, and in their participation in labor struggles throughout the Southwest. Radical community leaders like Magón defended the rights of immigrants while militant labor organizers protested unfair wages and terrible working conditions by engaging in unionization drives, labor strikes, and other actions.[5]

The radical tradition continued during the 1930s and 1940s but declined by the 1950s due to the anti-communist sentiment of those years. Three key organizations—El Congreso del Pueblo de Habla Española (Congress of Spanish-Speaking Peoples), ANMA, and Mine Mill—best represented this tradition during these years.[6]

El Congreso del Pueblo de Habla Española, or El Congreso for short, was formed in 1939 in Los Angeles. Although envisioned as a national organization, it functioned mostly in that city and was active for only a little more than a decade. Led by Josefina Fierro de Bright and Eduardo Quevedo, El Congreso protested anti-Mexican legislation in California, deportations of Mexican-origin workers and families, and police killings. It supported an expansion of relief programs, low-cost housing, bilingual education, desegregation, ethnic studies, and cultural activities for youth. It also supported women as leaders and members and fought for neutrality in international matters. Although El Congreso was part of a Mexican-origin leftist tradition, Mario García noted that it supported militant reform not revolution. This militant brand of politics also did not effectively challenge the dominance of middle-class organizations such as LULAC.[7]

After the bombing of Pearl Harbor, the organization's focus transformed from civil rights to the war effort. The struggle for civil rights continued, but it created tensions and undermined the campaign for unity. During the war, El Congreso opposed the Bracero Program and the *sinarquistas*, Spanish fascists who were blamed for undermining unity.[8]

In 1942 the organization disbanded, although Fierro de Bright and others continued to work in support of civil rights. Fierro de Bright, for instance, was responsible for establishing the Sleepy Lagoon Defense Committee in 1942.[9] At the end of the war, she voluntarily left the United States, fearing that she would be arrested.[10]

Another organization contributing to the radical tradition in Mexican American history was the International Union of Mine, Mill, and Smelter Workers. This union, referred to as the Mine Mill, was a founding partner of the radical Congress of Industrial Organizations (CIO), formed in 1936. The CIO focused on organizing unskilled workers and was more militant and progressive than the AFL.[11]

Mexican Americans and Mexican nationals employed at the American Smelting and Refining Company smelter and Phelps-Dodge refinery in El Paso formed a Mine Mill local in 1939 to represent the interests of workers in these two plants. Although the AFL was present there, it did not advocate for the interests of the Mexican and Mexican American workers, who constituted the vast majority of the workforce. The Mexican-origin workers, most of whom were unskilled, faced significant racial and class discrimination in these two plants. They were paid lower wages than Anglos, restricted to dead-end manual jobs, segregated at work, and excluded from more skilled and better paying jobs. They also faced terrible and unsafe working conditions and did not have any health benefits. Additionally, Mexican workers were forced to purchase overpriced provisions at the company store and lived in overcrowded and substandard homes next to the plant.[12]

The union faced many problems in recruiting members, given that a significant number resided in Mexico. It also faced growing hostility from plant officials and harassment by local law enforcement officials. Despite these difficulties, by 1942 Mine Mill had gained the support of a majority of workers in both plants. Several factors contributed to their success, including fiercely contesting the red-baiting charges of local officials, filing administrative complaints with federal agencies, solidarity with the labor movement in Mexico and the United States, and appeals to Mexican culture.[13]

In early 1946, the union called a strike at all eighteen American Smelting and Refining and Phelps-Dodge operations in the United States after both plants refused to meet its demands for a wage increase and for industry-wide bargaining. The two plants were willing to negotiate at the local level but not on an industry-wide basis. During the strike, the union established joint CIO relief committees to secure funds for strikers who were not allowed to work elsewhere or to receive unemployment benefits. It opened a soup kitchen and sought outside support. Mine Mill organizers also engaged in picketing on a few occasions. After four months of strikes and negotiations, the smelter and refinery agreed to increase wages, but did not concede to the demand for industry-wide bargaining. Although the union was successful in representing Mexican workers on both sides of the border and in securing wage increases during the 1940s, repressive actions during the Cold War years took a toll on the union in El Paso and throughout the Southwest. In 1950, it was expelled from the CIO because of its radicalism.[14]

A third radical Mexican American organization was ANMA, formed in 1949 by members of the Mine Mill union and supported by the Communist Party. Its purpose was to defend the cultural, political, and civil rights of Mexican nationals and Mexican Americans and to oppose all forms of discrimination on the basis of race, class, and gender. ANMA fiercely protested the popular stereotypes of Mexicans found in mainstream media. It also defended the cultural rights of Mexicans in the United States and promoted use of the Spanish language, along with Mexican music and cultural performances. Moreover, the organization protested deportations, police brutality, and red-baiting. Finally, ANMA strongly supported workers' struggles for unionization, fair wages, and better working conditions. Unlike in middle-class organizations such as LULAC, women played positive and visible roles in ANMA as evidenced by their appointment to national and local leadership positions from 1949 to 1952.[15]

During the Cold War the FBI investigated and harassed ANMA. It accused the organization of being a Communist Party front or at least being ideologically similar to the Communist Party because of

its support of workers and opposition to the war in Korea and the Cold
War in general. Attacks against the organization eventually led to its
demise in the 1950s.[16] Although repressed by Cold War politics, this
organization continued the legacy of the Mexican American radical and
leftist tradition in the United States. It fought for the interests of the
working class and against repression. Despite its radicalism, it mirrored
El Congreso and the Mine Mill union in that its basic aims were reform-
ist in nature and sought the full attainment by Mexican Americans of
democratic rights guaranteed in the U.S. Constitution.[17]

    Leftist organizations like Mine Mill and ANMA did not survive the
repressive environment of the Cold War. Thus, by the late 1950s no
significant organizations espousing militancy and radicalism existed
in the Mexican American community. That soon changed. In the 1960s
the radical and militant activist tradition reemerged as a few labor organizers and community activists formed new organizations to mobilize
Mexican Americans in the fields, countryside, and cities. The end of the
Bracero Program and of deportations in the early 1960s, accompanied
by the rise of a more activist federal government and civil rights movement, contributed to the surfacing of radical voices in the second half
of the 1960s.

    These new radical activists differed in several major ways from
the mainstream ones that espoused moderation in rhetoric and tactics. First, they did not look to the federal government to solve their
problems, nor did they seek recognition from the federal government.
Instead, they sought community empowerment and independent community activism. Second, they rejected the politics of the liberal agenda
and embraced militancy and direct-action tactics. In other words, they
rejected, questioned, or critiqued the Mexican American community's
predominant reliance on conventional methods of change. Although
tolerant of lobbying, negotiation, and litigation, the majority embraced
militancy, mass mobilization, marches, demonstrations, and boycotts as
legitimate means of struggle. Third, they questioned the culture of the
liberal agenda; that is, the expectation that Mexican Americans needed
to assimilate and abandon their home culture in order to succeed. For
these activists, the Spanish language, Mexican culture, and ethnic pride
were important ingredients of the struggle for social change. Finally,

they expanded the traditional concerns of the civil rights movement from seeking rights, recognition, and resources to include economic justice, return of stolen lands, feminism, urban discrimination, and educational inequity.

The radical voices of the 1960s laid the foundation for the later acceptance of cultural nationalism and feminism and for the emergence of the Chicano Movement. These activists inspired thousands of individuals, especially women and youth, to join La Causa (the cause) and provided different models of leadership for tackling issues of poverty, racism, sexism, and discrimination in American life. Who were these radicals and what actions did they take to inspire those who formed the Chicano Movement? Among the key activists were César Chávez, Dolores Huerta, Reies López Tijerina, Corky Gonzales, Francisca Flores, and a large number of college students, barrio youth, and high school students.

## CHÁVEZ, HUERTA, AND THE UNITED FARM WORKERS

Undoubtedly the most important catalyst for the Chicano Movement was César Chávez and the UFW labor union. Chávez was a soft-spoken activist who had been a migrant worker as a youth. In 1950 he joined the CSO. CSO chapters were involved in organizing local communities to improve their neighborhoods, tackle persistent problems like police brutality, and encourage greater involvement in the electoral arena. Chávez quickly moved up the ranks, becoming national director of CSO in 1960. Meanwhile, Dolores Huerta, born into an activist family in Dawson, New Mexico, had joined CSO in 1955 and helped mobilize communities to improve barrio conditions in Stockton, California.

In 1962, Chávez resigned as director after the CSO refused to support a program of organizing farmworkers. After his resignation, he moved to Delano, California. He soon persuaded several other individuals, including Dolores Huerta, to resign their positions in CSO and assist him in forming the National Farm Workers Association (NFWA). This organization later evolved into the UFW.[18]

The mission of NFWA was to organize agricultural farmworkers to fight for a union, increased wages, and better working conditions.

Farmworkers were the lowest paid workers in California and the most powerless workers in the country. They migrated from city to city, living in makeshift housing, earning starvation wages, and working under horrible conditions. They did not have a minimum wage, lacked basic amenities in the field, even restroom facilities and cold drinking water, and did not have any medical insurance.

The NFWA soon found itself embroiled in one of the largest and most contentious labor actions of this era: the California grape strike. On September 8, 1965, six hundred Filipino members of the Agricultural Workers Organizing Committee called a strike against table grape growers. When growers refused to negotiate with the union for a small, twenty-cent increase in hourly wages and improved working conditions, the Filipinos requested NFWA support. On September 16, 1965 (Mexican independence day), NFWA joined the strike and thousands walked out of the grape fields.[19] Opposed by some of the most powerful agricultural and political interests in the country and by many local communities, a NFWA-Filipino alliance mobilized thousands of farmworkers and engaged in a historic five-year strike.[20]

Before the strike began, Chávez obtained a commitment that the Filipinos would work together with Mexican farmworkers and would remain nonviolent. Over time, due to his fierce determination and commitment to nonviolence, Chávez came to dominate the strike and determine its course. "The first principle of non-violent action is that of non-cooperation with everything humiliating," Chávez proclaimed, quoting Mahatma Gandhi.[21] The strike drew widespread backing from outside California's Central Valley. Unions, church activists, college students, Latinos, other minorities, and civil rights groups all supported what became known as La Causa (the Cause), a broad, nonviolent movement for human dignity, civil rights, and economic justice.[22]

Soon after joining the strike NFWA called for a grape boycott. The absence of any progress by the following year motivated Chávez to lead a thirteen-day, 340-mile march from Delano to Sacramento. He aimed to pressure the growers and the state government to recognize the farmworkers' union and to bring widespread public attention to the farmworkers' cause. The march began on March 17, 1966; by the time it ended in Sacramento on March 30, a crowd of thousands had gathered.[23] In preparation for this march, the UFW, successor to the NFWA, issued El Plan de Delano, a manifesto calling for social justice for farmworkers and the creation of a new social order based on humanity, not profit.[24]

For their part, growers responded violently to the strike and boycott. First, they filed court injunctions to limit roadside picketing outside their properties. Second, they hired armed security guards, equipped foremen with shotguns, and engaged in a campaign of harassment. Some shot at unarmed picketers; tried to run them down with tractors, trucks, or cars; sprayed them with pesticides; threatened them with dogs, showered them with obscenities; and physically assaulted them. They also encouraged the formation of ad hoc organizations opposed to the farmworkers. Two such organizations that formed in Delano, the center of this organizing activity, were Mothers Against Chávez and Citizens for Facts. Finally, opponents of the farmworkers organized groups to counter-picket them carrying signs reading "Outsiders Go Home."[25]

Two years into the strike impatient strikers started agitating for violence against growers who abused them. Many equated nonviolence with inaction and even cowardice. To rededicate the movement to nonviolence, Chávez started a hunger strike in February 1968, losing thirty-five pounds in twenty-five days and causing his doctors to declare that his life was in danger. He did not end his fast until the workers quit all talk of violence. Senator Robert F. Kennedy was present when Chávez ended his hunger strike.[26]

In 1968, the UFW called for a nationwide boycott of table grapes. The boycott soon expanded internationally. For two years, thousands of individuals throughout the United States and Europe picketed local stores, held meetings to inform the public about the struggle for social justice, and encouraged local stores not to sell grapes and consumers not to eat them.[27] Despite the growers' violent responses to the union and the federal government's efforts to undermine it, this struggle continued until 1970, when growers caved in to the pressures of the boycott and public support for the farmworkers. In July of that year, the union obtained a series of favorable three-year contracts with most Central Valley table-grape growers.[28]

During this entire time, Dolores Huerta contributed significantly to the UFW movement. She recruited women to the cause, kept the union focused on nonviolent actions, and gained support for the grape boycott in the eastern United States. She also conducted pickets and actively engaged in boycott-related activities. Furthermore, she lobbied on behalf of the *huelga* (strike) and conducted successful negotiations with growers.[29]

This historic grape strike that started in 1965 and lasted until 1970 began as a limited effort to gain union recognition and wage increases in central California and involved a few hundred individuals. By the end of the decade it had grown into an international movement supported by thousands of people in the United States and abroad. The strike became something more than a campaign for union recognition and higher wages. It became a broad nonviolent crusade for social justice, human dignity, and civil rights.[30]

The UFW was not a typical union organized by outside professionals who relied on the strike and the picket line as their major weapons of struggle. Instead, it was organized by community activists who went beyond traditional union methods and used militancy, culture, music, religion, and civil rights tactics to reach their goals. The union was militant in its demands for collective bargaining, wage increases, and better working conditions. It bravely stood up to some of the most powerful economic and political forces in American life. The dates and actions the union chose reflected the militant history of Mexican Americans. For instance, the decision to join the Filipinos in a strike against grape growers took place on September 16, Mexican independence day. As the historian Ignacio M. García has noted, the use of a flag depicting a black eagle against a red background gave the movement an appearance of militancy. This symbol represented the farmworkers as active agents shaping their own destinies rather than passive victims of powerful growers.[31]

Unlike other contemporary organizations, the UFW incorporated working-class music and Mexican culture into organizing. They communicated in Spanish within the union at a time when it was illegal to use non-English languages in public life. In later years, it promoted a revitalization of Chicano vernacular speech, a hybrid, creative mixture of working-class English, Spanish, and *caló* (slang). Music and street theater served to entertain the farmworkers and to educate the public about its struggles. Luis Valdez joined La Causa soon after graduating from college. A creative young man, he was instrumental in the incorporation of music and culture into union activities.[32]

Like many other union members Valdez came from Delano and had worked in the fields as a youth. Since his public school days, Valdez had been interested in the arts, especially in puppetry and drama. He honed his drama skills in college and soon joined the San Francisco Mime Troupe, a well-known group engaged in political theater. In 1965, he joined the UFW and formed El Teatro Campesino, for which he created short one-act plays or skits around issues that farmworker-activists confronted on a daily basis. These skits ridiculed growers, dealt with the problems created by strikebreakers, and addressed strikers' fears.[33]

Valdez also incorporated music into these performances. Like many unions throughout history, the UFW already was using picket-line songs to unify its members in the fields and meeting halls. Valdez expanded the use of music to include a variety of Mexican songs, particularly *corridos* and *canciones*. Corridos are narrative ballads that typically tell the story of a folk hero and are sung to simple tunes. They emerged and proliferated during a time of profound and violent change along the Rio Grande and in South Texas between 1836 and the 1930s.[34] Canciones are traditional songs that deal with a variety of themes in Mexican history.[35] Songs such as "Viva la huelga" and "No nos moveran" (we shall not be moved) played crucial roles in inspiring UFW members and creating unity during their struggles.

Valdez's Teatro Campesino, with its songs and skits, was more than a form of entertainment that reflected farmworkers' struggles and inspired them to rejoice in their resistance. It was also a form of nonviolent cultural expression and protest. It served to educate a new generation of Mexican Americans—as well as Americans of all colors, genders, and creeds—about the plight and struggle of farmworkers. It was, in essence, an art that politicized and informed individuals about the importance of the movement.[36]

The union also used religious symbolism for inspiration. For instance, UFW members talked about participating in a pilgrimage or journey to social justice, sought penance in fighting against violence, prayed together in the fields, erected altars at union meetings, and displayed the flag of Our Lady of Guadalupe, the patron saint of Mexico and all Mexicans. In order to be inclusive it also displayed the Star of David during its rallies.

Valdez played a key role in promoting not only religious symbolism but also the rhetoric of revolution to expand the UFW's influence throughout the nation and in Latin America. An example of religious symbolism and the rhetoric of revolution in a nonviolent movement was El Plan de Delano, which he wrote. This proclamation, issued on the 340-mile march to Sacramento, made several important points. First, it declared that this action was the beginning of a social movement for economic justice. Second, it sought support from all political groups throughout the land and from the U.S. government, "which is also our government." Third, it sought the active participation of all major religions in the country and carried flags of Our Lady of Guadalupe, the Sacred Cross, and the Star of David to demonstrate that they were not "sectarians." Fourth, it declared that farmworkers were suffering and were not afraid to suffer further "in order to win our cause." Fifth, it declared that it would unite all poor people and people of color in support of the farmworkers' cause. Finally, it would strike in order to pursue a peaceful revolution that would lead to a new social order.[37]

The UFW went beyond conventional tactics and used militancy and direct action in its struggle for economic justice. In addition to huelgas and picket lines, it organized protest marches, economic boycotts, demonstrations, and mass mobilizations. Inspired by Dr. Martin Luther King and Mahatma Gandhi, Chávez introduced a philosophy of nonviolence into union activities. He engaged in a hunger strike as a way of rededicating the workers to nonviolence. Finally, the union was highly patriotic at a time when many Americans were burning the flag to protest the war in Vietnam. It displayed the Mexican and U.S. flags at all of its activities, along with the union's black eagle flag. In later years, the UFW flag became one of the most recognized symbols of the Chicano Movement.

## REIES LÓPEZ TIJERINA AND THE LAND
## GRANT MOVEMENT

Another grassroots activist who emerged in this period was Reies López Tijerina. Trained as a Pentecostal preacher, Tijerina worked to mobilize land-grant heirs in New Mexico who had lost their land to Anglo settlers in the nineteenth century and to the federal government in the twentieth. In August 1962, while living in Albuquerque, Tijerina drafted the first plan of the Alianza Federal de las Mercedes (Federal Land Grant Alliance), then in October issued a letter calling for an Alianza of Pueblos and Pobladores (Alliance of Towns and Settlers). La Alianza was officially incorporated on February 2, 1963, the 115th anniversary of the signing of the Treaty of Guadalupe Hidalgo, which ceded Mexican land to the United States with a promise that Mexican land-grant holders would retain their property. Tijerina was elected president and Eduardo Chávez vice-president.[38]

La Alianza sought to organize the heirs to all Spanish land grants covered by the Treaty of Guadalupe Hidalgo and acquaint them with their rights. He argued that through fraud, deception, and other extralegal means, Anglos and the U.S. government had unlawfully dispossessed them of their communal lands. The group further sought to foster pride in the heritage of the Native New Mexicans. Tijerina felt that Anglos had erased the history of the Indian, Spanish, and Mexican peoples who had preceded them and had sought to suppress the Spanish language, which had been spoken in New Mexico since the 1500s. Unlike other Mexican American leaders, Tijerina argued that the Mexican population was native to the region, because they were Indo-Hispanos, the offspring of Spaniards and Indians. The issue for La Alianza, then, was not merely land dispossession but also cultural suppression. Their struggle was aimed at demanding the restoration of their land and full civil and cultural rights.[39]

In the early 1960s Tijerina used traditional methods to gain recognition of the land grant issue. He unsuccessfully petitioned various government officials for redress, lobbied legislators to address the concerns of these landless individuals, and filed lawsuits. By the mid-1960s, he began to take more forceful action. In October 1966, more than three hundred Alianza members occupied Echo Amphitheater Park, located in the Carson National Forest, which had been part of a communal grant known as the San Joaquín del Río de Chama. The Alianza moved in and proclaimed an independent nation, the Republic of San Joaquín del Río de Chama. Alianza members, many of them descendants of the original settlers, elected officials and issued visas to passing tourists. Two forest rangers who attempted to remove the protesters were arrested by the newly elected marshals. The rangers were tried, convicted of trespassing, given suspended sentences, and released along with their trucks.[40]

After occupying the park for five days, the Aliancistas turned themselves in. Five of the occupiers, including Reies and his brother Cristóbal were charged with assault on the rangers and with converting government property to personal use. Bail was set at $5,000 apiece. Tijerina hoped to go to trial in order to publicly address the theft of the communal lands.[41]

In 1967, some of his followers tried to make a citizens' arrest of Rio Arriba County district attorney Alfonso Sánchez for obstructing their efforts to mobilize.[42] A shootout ensued in which one person was killed. The lieutenant governor called out the National Guard with tanks and weapons in an effort to capture Tijerina and his supporters. Several weeks later, Tijerina turned himself in, but neither he nor his group stopped fighting for their cause.[43]

Unlike most Chicano leaders, Tijerina sought alliances with militant blacks, Native Americans, and other oppressed groups.[44] More importantly, he sought to become the national leader of the growing Mexican American movement in the Southwest. He organized several youth conferences in 1966 and 1967 to publicize the land grant struggle in New Mexico and encourage youth to organize on a regional basis and take pride in their heritage. Youth responded to his calls, and soon they proposed a regional form of communication, the establishment of a national party, the promotion of Mexican culture, and pride in being of Mexican descent.[45]

Tijerina was no ordinary organizer. He expanded the struggle to include cultural rights, especially the rights to speak Spanish and preserve their way of life. He used all forms of direct action, including violence, to reach his goals. Finally, he inspired young people and sought to educate them about the land grant struggle, the effort to preserve Spanish, and the need to acknowledge their indigenous heritage. In sum, Tijerina fought for the rights of those dispossessed of their lands and culture and sought to influence young militants throughout the Southwest eager for a more aggressive style of leadership.

## CORKY GONZALES AND THE CRUSADE FOR JUSTICE

Another important grassroots activist who emerged in this period was Rodolfo "Corky" Gonzales from Denver, Colorado. During the early and mid-1960s Gonzales began to organize Mexican American parents and youth to tackle a variety of urban issues, such as police brutality, civil rights, discrimination in the schools, and a loss of identity among young people.

Before his community activism, Gonzales had been a well-known boxer and a Mexican American liberal very much involved in mainstream political activities at the local and national levels. Disgusted with electoral politics, he resigned from the Democratic Party in 1965 and formed the Crusade for Justice. For several years, he engaged in rallies and demonstrations against police brutality, racism, and discrimination in the city. In 1967, he wrote *I Am Joaquín*, a historically based epic poem about the Mexican American community's struggle for economic survival and its loss of identity due to assimilation. This poem became one of the most important documents of the Chicano Movement.[46]

One year later, in 1968, he attended the Poor People's Campaign in Washington, DC, and emerged as a national leader effectively representing the interests and desires of a broad spectrum of Mexican Americans in the Southwest. Tijerina also attended this event, but he was narrowly focused on the land grant issue.[47] While not ignoring this issue, Gonzales also addressed problems of education, employment, and identity. While at the Poor People's Campaign, he issued El Plan del Barrio, an eight-point manifesto for combating the complex problems confronting the Mexican American community. This plan demanded a more inclusive and community-based public school system that would be free, bilingual, bicultural, and caring. It called for housing that was safe, based on family needs, and equipped with recreational spaces for children and youth. Another point was the return of stolen lands and compensation for those who had lost them. Job training and placement programs for better employment opportunities, investigations of police brutality, promotion of court reforms, and Mexican American ownership of businesses serving the community were other goals. Likewise, it demanded a redistribution of wealth and additional land reforms.[48]

Gonzales would assume a more important role in the Chicano Movement by 1969 with the establishment of the Chicano Youth Liberation Conferences and the promotion of nationalism throughout the country.

## FRANCISCA FLORES AND THE LEAGUE OF MEXICAN AMERICAN WOMEN

Another group illustrating the new approach to organizing was the League of Mexican American Women. For more than a decade the League inspired hundreds of Mexican American women to take independent actions on matters of great concern to them. In contrast to the male-dominated organizations of the mid-1960s, the League simultaneously contested both racism and sexism. This organization predated the better-known radical activist organizations of the 1960s and is usually not included in histories of the Mexican American civil rights movement. But the League deserves to be included because it took a new approach to community organizing that was soon reflected in the actions of the UFW, La Alianza, and the Crusade for Justice.

The League of Mexican American Women was founded by two dynamic Mexican American women, Francisca Flores and Ramona Tijerina Morin. Flores was born in San Diego in 1913. As a young child she heard many stories of daring men and women who fought in the Mexican Revolution. These stories inspired and motivated her to organize other women who had survived the revolution and were now living in southern California.[49] During the early 1940s she moved to Los Angeles and started getting involved in Mexican American causes, including the Sleepy Lagoon Defense Committee (a multiracial community-based group dedicated to freeing the twelve Mexican American young men who had been falsely convicted of the 1942 murder of José Gallardo

Díaz) and ANMA (formed in 1949). During the 1950s she spoke out against the House Committee on Un-American Activities and helped cofound the CSO and MAPA. Her involvement in CSO and MAPA convinced her that the men in these organizations did not accept women as equals or value their contributions. She once told her nephew, "I knew that the men [in Mexican American organizations] didn't take us seriously. They only wanted us to make tortillas. They couldn't accept that we had our own ideas."[50] Mexican American male leaders also failed to recognize the important role women played in electoral campaigns and refused to elect women to executive positions in their organizations. No woman, for instance, was elected as president or vice-president of CSO or MAPA during the 1950s.[51]

Morin was born in Missouri in 1919 but raised in Los Angeles. She and her husband, a World War II hero and well-known author, joined CSO and helped organize chapters of both the AGIF and LULAC during the 1940s and 1950s. Morin, like Flores, played a key role in organizing Ladies Auxiliary chapters for both organizations.[52]

Gender inequities in Mexican American civil rights organizations motivated Flores and Morin to create a separate, independent activist organization that would empower women and both value and recognize their accomplishments. Positive experiences with women's organizations like the Young Women's Christian Association and the LULAC and AGIF Ladies Auxiliaries persuaded them this would be a more appropriate course than fighting for recognition in male-dominated environments. The League, formed in 1958, provided an alternative political space where Mexican American women did not have to deal with the "macho" attitudes of men. It engaged in several important activities during the 1960s. First, it staged political forums where Mexican American women could come together to discuss local, state, and national elections; how to combat racism; and how to increase civic involvement of League members. Second, it hosted social events to support candidates running for office, endorsed them during elections, and campaigned for them. The League, for instance, campaigned for the congressional races of George Brown Jr. and Edward Roybal in 1962. Political leaders in the Democratic Party saw the value of the League's work and by the early 1960s actively sought its support.[53] Third, the League organized annual achievement award banquets from 1960 to 1969 to publicly acknowledge the value and significance of Mexican American women's contributions to society and to the movement. At each event two women received the League's Outstanding Achievement Award and twenty-five received the Honor Roll Award for making a difference in their communities. These recognitions challenged the dominant society's stereotypes of Mexican American women as non-achievers and as passive and uninvolved. In total, more than 250 women from California and the Southwest were recognized for their accomplishments during the 1960s. The criteria for the awards were active participation in shaping public policy, influence on future generations of Mexican Americans, and support for the feminist agenda. Fourth, the League pressured local officials to appoint Mexican American women to positions in city government or to federal positions at the local level.[54]

In 1963, Flores and a friend, Delfino Varela, founded a bimonthly editorial and informational newsletter called *Carta Editorial*, aimed at providing an alternative, feminist perspective on Mexican American politics. This newsletter became an important tool for keeping readers abreast of political developments in the community and for exposing the hypocrisy of male leaders in the Mexican American civil rights movement.[55]

The emphasis of the League was on empowering women in the context of sexism in the Mexican American civil rights movement and on providing them opportunities to come together and solve their own problems without the presence of men who refused to acknowledge or value their capabilities. Like other later groups, it encouraged self-determination, problem solving, and independent political action. These qualities became integral elements of Chicano Movement ideals and behaviors in the 1970s and were soon reflected in other well-known organizations like the UFW, La Alianza, and the Crusade for Justice.[56]

## YOUTH

The final set of grassroots activists laying the groundwork for the emergence of the Chicano Movement were young people, especially college students, barrio youth, and high school students. Students formed a variety of organizations on college campuses in the mid-1960s while non-college youths formed barrio organizations to confront the racism and discrimination they encountered on a daily basis in their community.

College students began to organize in the mid-1960s as they gained a presence in universities. A hostile racial climate in majority white institutions, a desire to preserve their identities, and their isolation on campus due to low enrollment rates motivated them to organize. In these years, college youth focused their energies on organizational matters, on clarifying their goals, and on supporting a few community struggles, especially the UFW. Two of the most important groups that formed in this period were United Mexican American Students (UMAS) in California and the Mexican American Youth Organization (MAYO) in Texas.[57]

Young people in the community likewise focused on getting organized, on increasing their awareness about public issues, and on improving their leadership capabilities. One of the most important barrio groups that formed during this period was the Brown Berets, who could be found in various states but were concentrated in California. Barrio youth in Texas, unlike their counterparts in California and other states, generally joined a chapter of MAYO. These young people were engaged in promoting reforms in the community, fighting police brutality, opposing the war in Vietnam, and supporting high school student walkouts.[58]

Student and barrio activists, in general, did not readily accept the moderate liberal agenda nor did they embrace its politics and culture. The majority believed in direct action and were critical of assimilation, integration, and political leaders like President Johnson. They also criticized existing Mexican American organizations and leaders as too timid in their approach to activism. Phil Castruita, a California State College UMAS member, expressed this sentiment well at the October 1967 Cabinet Committee Hearings when he said, "The young chicanos [*sic*] see this conference as the last chance you older chicanos have to come through." "If nothing happens from this," he added, "you'll have to step aside or we'll walk over you."

The October 1967 Inter-Agency Committee on Mexican-American Affairs hearings provided a national forum for college students and barrio youth to act on their beliefs. College students, encouraged by Tijerina, Gonzales, and other radicals, emerged as important national actors when they decided to picket the Cabinet Committee Hearings. On the second day of the hearings, the youth joined the more radical members of established Mexican American organizations to boycott the hearings and hold their own counter-conference in the barrios of El Paso.[59]

High school students also emerged as important actors in the emerging Chicano Movement when thousands of them walked out of public schools to protest inadequate and inferior conditions. The first large walkout took place in East Los Angeles on March 1, 1968. On this date and for several additional days, thousands of Mexican American students walked out of the Los Angeles public schools to challenge their second-class treatment by educators. The boycotts dramatized some of the most blatant forms of discrimination against students. Among the key policies and practices they challenged were prejudicial and insensitive teachers; bans on speaking Spanish; exclusion of Mexican culture from the curriculum; failure to hire Mexican American teachers, counselors, and other professional staff; and lack of student rights.[60]

The walkouts, or "blowouts" as they were called, were inspired by Sal Castro, a charismatic history teacher at Lincoln High School. He encouraged students to challenge authorities and take a risk in order to improve their schools.[61] These actions, as Carlos Muñoz Jr. noted in the early 1970s, had a profound effect on the politics of the Mexican American community and ignited the urban aspect of the Chicano Movement. The blowouts also significantly influenced students. Those who participated in them acquired a renewed sense of empowerment and faith in their abilities to promote social and educational change.[62]

School walkouts soon spread to other parts of the country, such as Denver, Colorado, and Chicago, Illinois.[63] The majority of them took place in Texas. The first walkout in that state took place in San Antonio in May 1968, but the most dramatic one occurred in the Edcouch-Elsa School District in mid-November of that year.[64] The most influential and controversial one took place in Crystal City. From 1968 to 1972 high school students in Texas conducted more than thirty-nine walkouts.[65] The walkouts took place for several reasons. Among the most important were underlying patterns of racial discrimination, inferior school conditions, and exclusionary school policies and practices. Active mobilization by community political organizations, as several authors

have noted, also played an important part in encouraging students to
walk out of the public schools.[66]

Although aimed at bringing about important changes, not all walkouts
were successful in accomplishing their goals. Those in San Antonio and
Kingsville, Texas, for instance, did not lead to any significant reform
of the schools.[67] Those in Los Angeles, California, had mixed results.
The student protests served to publicize the plight of Chicana/o schooling and to momentarily foment community militancy and political
mobilization, but they failed to produce significant structural change
in education. After the walkouts Mexican Americans continued to be
powerless and their schools continued to be inferior. The walkouts in
Los Angeles led to significant short-term changes in the Mexican American community but not in the public schools.[68] The walkouts in Rancho
Cucamonga, California, as well as Crystal City, Houston, Uvalde, and
Edcouch-Elsa, Texas, did lead to significant changes in the schools and
in the social and political environment.[69]

Despite the mixed results of student actions, the walkouts inspired
thousands of young people to envision a world where their heritage would
be recognized, their academic needs met, and their dignity respected.
Student walkouts might not have immediately changed the structure
or conditions of schooling, but they definitely changed the political
dynamics of the Mexican-origin community and the consciousness of
the students who participated in them. These actions empowered them,
increasing their awareness of oppression, of who they were, and of their
potential for initiating significant change through collective action.

By 1968, significant mobilization had been undertaken by a new generation of activists interested in empowering the community and in using
both culture and direct action tactics to bring about significant change
in American society rather than depending on the federal government
to resolve their problems of powerlessness and poverty. The following
year, Corky Gonzales made plans to unify the growing numbers of
young people involved in social change around nationalist ideals. His
intervention led to the emergence of the Chicano Movement. The next
chapter will focus on the making of the nationalist identity and on the
character of this movement.

## CHAPTER 3

# Radicals and the Chicano Movement, 1969–1978

By 1968 significant numbers of Mexican Americans were involved in protest activities throughout the Southwest. Thousands joined La Causa and supported the farmworker, land grant, and urban struggles of the Crusade for Justice. Many others also supported young people's advocacy for more relevant experiences in higher education, improved conditions in the barrios, and better public schools throughout the country. This explosion of activity occurred in the context of tremendous social and political ferment in the nation and throughout the world.

Despite the increase in activism, there was no national Chicano Movement yet. Instead there were separate struggles rooted in local or state conditions. There was a farmworker movement, a land grant movement, a women's movement, and a student movement. But there was no sense of a "Chicano" movement per se. Activists, for the most part, did not have a Chicana or Chicano identity. They had a Mexican American identity, an Indo-Hispano identity, or a variety of other identities, but not a Chicano one.

A national Chicano identity did not emerge until 1969. In this year Corky Gonzales convened the first National Chicano Youth Liberation Conference in Denver. Gonzales sought to unify the young activists under the rubric of what he called nationalism and to provide direction to those involved in these efforts. His focus was on young activists, whom he felt could destroy a system that was rotten to the core.[1] Cultural nationalism surfaced at this conference and became the guiding ideology for young activists throughout the country. The promotion of nationalism among these activists contributed significantly to the development of

the Chicano identity. A second conference in Santa Barbara a month later
also contributed to the development of a common identity by endorsing
the use of the term "Chicano" for activists in general and Movimiento
Estudiantil Chicano de Aztlán, or MEChA, for student activists in particular. Although cultural nationalism was a key ingredient of Chicano
identity, it was not the only one. Feminism, Marxism, internationalism
or anticolonialism, and liberalism were other important elements of this
identity.

   This chapter provides an interpretation of this radical movement. It
focuses on the making of the nationalist identities that guided its activities and on the major types of struggles in which activists engaged during the movement's most important years, from 1969 to 1978. I argue
that the Chicano Movement was ideologically diverse and revolved
around four major concerns: class, race, gender, and culture. This movement, I might note, also temporarily drowned out the voices of moderate activists who still believed in the liberal agenda and in the politics
of peaceful change.


## MULTIPLE NATIONALISMS IN THE MAKING
## OF THE CHICANO IDENTITY

The Chicano Movement was a complex series of radical actions that
originated in the late 1960s in response to a variety of social and political developments in the Mexican American community and in society
at large. Among the most important factor instigating this movement
was the emergence of a new group of grassroots activists in the second
half of the 1960s who rejected the liberal agenda of moderate Mexican
American activists, introduced new forms of struggle in the community, and inspired hundreds of individuals of different ages and genders
to become involved in La Causa.[2] Other factors that played key roles
in the origins of the Chicano Movement included federal activism, the
Black civil rights movement, the counterculture, the antiwar protests,
the international student movement, and the third world struggles
against colonialism.[3]

   The movement's guiding ideology was cultural nationalism. This
ideology emerged at the first National Chicano Youth Liberation

Conference called by Corky Gonzales. More than 1,500 young activists attended this conference held at the Crusade for Justice headquarters in March 1969. For several days the attendees debated how they should organize, who should be involved, what direction the emerging activism should take, and what ideologies should guide this movement.[4]

A major result of this conference was the development of El Plan de Aztlán. This document reflected the new ethnic consciousness of the youth activists who met in Denver, which was promoted by the Crusade for Justice. The plan had two major parts, a preamble and a plan of action. The preamble appropriated the rhetoric of anticolonial struggles in Africa, Asia, and Latin America to interpret the historical and contemporary experiences of Chicanos in the United States. The literature on anticolonial struggles spoke about the colonizer-colonized relationship, the exploitation of the colony's resources, the repression of the colonizer's cultural traditions and identities, and the need to gain independence and control of their own nation-state.[5]

Many of these anticolonial ideas were reflected in El Plan de Aztlán. The preamble, for instance, portrayed Chicanos as a nation of indigenous and mestizo heritage that had been invaded and conquered by Anglo colonizers. This is reflected in the very first clause: "In the spirit of a new people that is conscious not only of its proud historical heritage, but also of the brutal 'Gringo' invasion of our territories." The document goes on to describe the responsibility and destiny of those who were "inhabitants and civilizers of the northern land of Aztlan." Aztlán was the mythical home of the Nahua Indians, commonly known as the Aztecs. Chicano activists interpreted that home to be in the U.S. Southwest. Part of the destiny of Chicanos, the preamble continued, was to unite on the basis of love and brotherhood and struggle against the "foreigner 'Gabacho,' who exploits our riches and destroys our culture."[6]

The final statements make three points. The first declares the independence of "our Mestizo Nation" from the "Gringo" colonizer. The second reiterates the idea that Chicanos are a "Bronze People with a Bronze Culture." The third declares to all concerned that Chicanos are a part of the nation of Aztlán: "Before the world, before all of North America, before all our brothers in the Bronze Continent, We are a Nation. We are a Union of free pueblos, We are Aztlan."[7]

The plan also recommended a host of actions to achieve Chicano self-determination and liberation in the United States. First, it stipulated that nationalism was the means for organizing the community to fight for total liberation from oppression and exploitation.[8] Second, it listed seven organizational goals for the activists to pursue: (1) encourage unity among all Chicanos, (2) gain control of all economic institutions in the barrio, (3) control and make education relevant for Chicanos, (4) make all institutions serve the needs of the community, (5) engage in self-defense of the community, (6) promote Chicano cultural values to defeat the Anglo capitalist value system, and (7) establish an independent political party to achieve political liberation. Third, it presented an action plan listing five specific things that all Chicanos should do. Two of these were distributing El Plan de Aztlán throughout the land and calling for a national walkout on September 16 (16 de septiembre, Mexican independence day) until all the demands for school reforms were met. The fourth point reiterated the importance and significance of liberation. Once liberated from gringo control, it stipulated, the nation of Aztlán would be free to make its own decisions "on the usage of our lands, the taxation of our goods, the utilization of our bodies for war, the determination of justice (reward and punishment), and the profit of our sweat."[9]

El Plan de Aztlán became a call to action on the basis of nationalism and a national plan for Chicano liberation.[10] The following month large numbers of faculty, students, staff, and grassroots leaders met at the University of California, Santa Barbara, to discuss issues Mexican Americans confronted at the postsecondary level and to develop strategies for resolving them. After attendees discussed these concerns, they issued what came to be known as *El Plan de Santa Barbara: A Chicano Plan for Higher Education*. This document, adopted in April 1969, assessed the role that universities could play in promoting social change, and how students, faculty, staff, and community members could further this process.[11]

The plan for higher education began with a short manifesto which argued that self-determination was the only acceptable way to achieve Chicano liberation in higher education. Additionally, it outlined proposals for establishing Chicano studies departments; for recruiting

Chicano students, faculty, and staff to the university; for ensuring that the Chicano community maintained control of these departments; and for maintaining Chicano political independence on campus. The plan called for the adoption of a new name for student organizations and for community activists. Student groups would be called Movimiento Estudiantil Chicano de Aztlán and youth activists would be known as Chicanos. The former would help promote unity among student activists across the country, the latter would reflect the new identity of these activists.[12]

In 1970 and 1971, Corky Gonzales organized the second and third National Chicano Youth Liberation Conferences to discuss further actions that young people could take to promote what he called the liberation of the Chicano community. A host of resolutions on many concerns were issued during these events.[13]

During the late 1960s and early 1970s activists and scholars also published a large number of articles and books providing their own interpretations and meanings of the Chicano Movement in general and the ideas embodied in these plans and resolutions in particular. Corky Gonzales, José Ángel Gutiérrez, Enriqueta Longeaux y Vásquez, and many others sought to clarify, elaborate, or explain the meaning of concepts such as Aztlán, nationalism, Chicano cultural values, and Chicana liberation.[14]

The various documents drafted and resolutions passed at the national conferences, as well as personal statements and writings published over the next several years, became the ideological basis for the Chicano Movement. Chicanismo, or the web of ideologies and behaviors guiding movement activists, was a new political consciousness that emphasized race, class, gender, and culture within the context of an oppressive society. The Chicano identity and its attendant behaviors, as Ignacio M. García noted, "marked a transformation in the way Mexican Americans thought about themselves, enabling them for the first time to see themselves as a community with a past and a present."[15] It allowed Chicanos to view themselves not as immigrants and white but as native and brown. Chicanos were mestizos and had Native American roots. Their ancestors were the Aztecs who lived in Aztlán. And Aztlán, Chicanos argued, was located in the Southwest. This ideology also encouraged activists to view Mexican-origin individuals not as free and passive but as colonized and exploited.[16] Gringos had invaded their territory, exploited their labor, and destroyed their culture, Chicanos argued.

The preamble to El Plan de Aztlán described Chicanos as mostly a working-class population. Individuals like Luis Valdez and Juan Gómez-Quiñones supported this idea and argued that activists should work for the betterment of the working class. At the same time, however, the plan argued that nationalism committed "all levels of Chicano society—the barrio, the campo, the ranchero, the writer, the teacher, the worker, [and] the professional—to la Causa."[17]

Chicanismo also meant that nationalists were proud of their heritage and their Bronze culture, as noted in El Plan. These concepts were later defined as meaning their ethnicity and culture, especially its values emphasizing family, humanism, language, and cooperation. Finally, El Plan stated that Chicanos were a nation within the United States. They were the nation of Aztlán. In response to the oppression they faced as a nation, they were declaring their independence from the colonizer in order to determine their own destiny. In addition to these nationalist ideas, Chicanismo also embraced a new form of struggle based on several key behaviors. First, it would be militant and aggressive. Second, it would foment rapid social change and different degrees of social change. Finally, it would be based on direct action tactics such as protest, demonstrations, and mass mobilization.[18]

## OTHER IDEOLOGIES

Cultural nationalism was not the only ideology represented at the Denver conference. So were feminism and Marxism, but they were both suppressed by the majority of those present. Feminism was discussed at a panel on the concerns of Chicanas in the Chicano Movement. Those present argued that one of the key issues confronting Chicanas was sexism: Chicano men were oppressing them, blocking them from full participation in leadership roles, and ignoring their concerns.[19] The majority resolved to encourage Chicanas to participate at all levels of the struggle, to educate other women about the issues in the movement, to encourage self-determination among themselves, to encourage both men and women to assume greater responsibility in the family, and to include all these ideas in the formation of La Raza Unida Party.[20] Some panel members argued that talk of feminism and Chicana liberation was divisive and that, for the sake of unity, women should stand with the men "against the gabacho system."[21]

Despite the consensus of the Chicana panel, the conference participants rejected a resolution acknowledging women's issues and concerns. Instead participants passed a resolution stating that Chicanas did not want to separate themselves from Chicanos but rather wanted "to strengthen and free our nation of Aztlan."[22] Most Chicanas interpreted this resolution as stipulating that they did not want to be liberated at this time.[23] Undeterred, they developed their feminist ideology in the months after the Denver conference. Organizing caucuses within Chicano organizations or forming their own groups, they used print media, discussion groups, and other means to raise awareness about their subordinate status in the movement and the need to promote feminism.[24]

Marxism likewise emerged at the Denver conference but was also suppressed by Corky Gonzales and other cultural nationalists. Marxists were quite diverse in their beliefs, following variously the ideas of Karl Marx, V. I. Lenin, Joseph Stalin, and Mao Zedong, among others. Collectively, they argued that cultural nationalism was reactionary and served to mask the source of Chicano oppression. They challenged the romantic and idealistic notion of cultural nationalism and its emphasis on racial oppression and racial conflict, arguing that this concept hid the true nature of oppression in America.[25] For these activists, class—not culture, race, or gender—was the primary culprit in the oppression of the Chicano community.[26]

Despite its suppression, Marxism continued to be an important ideology in the movement. During the first half of the 1970s, it was articulated by Chicano members of majority white organizations such as the Socialist Workers Party (SWP), the Young Socialist Alliance (YSA), and the Communist Party, USA. By the latter part of the decade, a few Chicano-based Marxist organizations, including the Centro de Acción Social Autónoma (CASA) and the August 29th Movement (ATM), promoted distinct forms of Marxism and nationalism in the community.

Like other Marxist organizations, they sought to gain leadership of activist organizations in particular and of the Chicano Movement in general.

Another influential ideological strand present at the Denver conference and in the Chicano Movement was internationalism. George Mariscal argues that this type of nationalism was based on anticolonialism and the struggles by developing ("third world") countries against colonialism. El Plan de Aztlán reflected many of these ideas. Unlike cultural nationalism, which focused on promoting pride and unity in Mexican heritage in the United States, anticolonialism linked local struggles against discrimination to global struggles against colonialism in the developing world. Some individuals referred to this as Third Worldism or anticolonialism.[27]

Finally, liberalism, while not articulated at the Denver conference, was very much present in the Mexican American community throughout the Southwest. Gonzales himself had believed in liberalism in the early 1960s. Although he and many young people officially rejected liberalism by the late 1960s, activists at the conference and in the community in general continued to have faith in this ideology. Those who believed in liberal ideas of moderate and gradual change soon formed a variety of organizations that supported and collaborated with more radical Chicano activists. Among these new organizations were the Mexican American Legal Defense and Education Fund (MALDEF), the Southwest Council of La Raza, and the Southwest Voter Registration Education Project (SVREP). Liberalism, in other words, did not die out during the Chicano Movement era. It continued to have significant influence on activists and on the movement.

Even within the ideological strands of the Chicano Movement, activists' beliefs were not monolithic. Each ideology was composed of diverse and at times contrasting ideas. For instance, different forms of Marxism were found in the Chicano Movement, with the SWP and the YSA having many advocates. These groups believed in Trotskyism, a particular form of radical thought as interpreted by Leon Trotsky. The Chicano-based ATM believed in Marxism-Leninism-Maoism, a distinct ideology embodying the ideas of these three major Marxists. Still others adhered to other forms of Marxism as interpreted by scholars and revolutionaries throughout the world and in the United States.[28]

The presence and acceptance of diverse ideological strands within activist communities led to the emergence of different types of nationalism in the Chicano Movement. These nationalisms—known by various names, such as cultural, liberal, feminist, revolutionary, and Marxist—either rejected all forms of "gringo" ideology or else they incorporated selective aspects of liberal, feminist, internationalist, or Marxist ones. The diversity of nationalist thought led to conflict, tensions, and clashes between many activists and between numerous activist organizations involved in community struggles. Personality styles, individual egos, desire for power, and government repression also contributed to tensions within Chicano Movement organizations and in struggles for social justice. At times, nationalists, feminists, Marxists, internationalists, and even liberals worked together. At other times they clashed over goals, strategies, and tactics. In a few cases, each faction worked independently.

## THE CHICANO MOVEMENT

The Chicano Movement was a multifaceted fight against many forms of social injustice and inequity. Although Chicana and Chicano activists engaged in countless struggles, the majority revolved around four basic concerns: class, race, gender, and culture. The following elaborates on these types of struggles.

## *Class*

The historian Ignacio M. García noted in his book *Chicanismo* that during the late 1960s and the 1970s Chicano activists, intellectuals, and artists rediscovered pride in their community, racial origins, and working-class status. Emphasis on the last quickly led activists to direct their reform efforts toward improving the material conditions of Mexican immigrant and Mexican American workers. It also led to the development of a positive image of working-class communities, individuals, and cultures, as well as the affirmation of values associated with the masses of people living in barrios throughout the country.[29]

This renewed pride in the working-class Mexican-origin community led Chicano Movement activists to support a large number of worker struggles. Among the most important was the movement initiated by the UFW in California, in which Chicano activists, especially students, played key roles. In the early years of the strike, student-activists provided entertainment, marched with Chávez, attended rallies in various cities, and served on boycott committees throughout the country. By the late 1960s, student groups such as MEChA and MAYO picketed stores throughout the country in support of the UFW boycott, raised funds for the union, and agitated in Mexican American communities on behalf of the union's struggle for recognition, higher wages, and improved working conditions.

Chicano Movement activists did not limit themselves to supporting rural farmworkers' efforts to unionize and gain better working conditions. They also supported a variety of worker struggles in cities and universities. One of the most important such actions during the 1970s was the Farah strike in El Paso.[30] In 1972, Mexican American women members of the Amalgamated Clothing Workers of America struck several Farah Manufacturing Company plants. The company was one of the major employers in the city. The garment workers sought increased wages, improvement in health and safety conditions, and elimination of harassment and racism from male supervisors. When the company refused to negotiate with the garment workers, the union called for a national boycott of Farah products. Thousands of consumers, including Chicana and Chicano activists, responded to the call. Some marched on the garment workers' behalf while others agitated and disseminated information about the important struggle for economic justice being waged by mostly Mexican American women workers. The determination of the women and the support from masses of people eventually forced the company to negotiate with the union and to grant important concessions.[31]

Chicana and Chicano student activists on several university campuses sometimes supported or led efforts to improve the wages and working conditions of workers employed by local businesses. The actions of the Mexican American Student Organization (MASO) at Arizona State University (ASU) in Tempe illustrates the role movement activists played in supporting these types of local working-class struggles. MASO was formed at ASU in 1968 in order to "sensitize Mexican

Americans to the Chicano movement."[32] It fought for the establishment of Chicano studies; the hiring of Chicano faculty, administrators, and staff; and the creation of student support services at ASU. It also supported the farmworker movement and fought to improve the working conditions of Mexican American wage earners. During the 1968–69 school year, for instance, MASO demanded that ASU terminate its contract with Phoenix Linen and Towel Supply Company and its laundry division, Bell Laundry. According to MASO, the local company discriminated against its mostly Mexican-origin workers, paid low wages, and had inferior working conditions. MASO researched the company, obtained support from more than one hundred campus organizations, and pressured the Arizona Civil Rights Commission and the EEOC to investigate the mistreatment of Mexican American workers at Bell Laundry. MASO also educated the university community about the company's discriminatory practices, held rallies in support of the workers, and met with the university president to demand action. By 1969, the EEOC, the Civil Rights Commission, and even ASU administrators acknowledged that the linen company discriminated against the laundry workers. In order not to lose its contract with ASU, the company improved the wages and working conditions of its Mexican American employees. MASO's efforts in this case led to important advances in the status of laundry workers in the local community.[33]

MASO continued its campaign against discrimination at ASU. In 1973, the student organization, now known as MEChA, initiated a new effort against employment discrimination on campus. It filed a class-action lawsuit against the ASU administration alleging a "pattern of discrimination" against Mexican American employees at the university. Chicano faculty and staff joined Mexican American community organizations to file their own employment discrimination lawsuit two years later. Chicano activists conducted rallies at the university, pressured the EEOC to conduct another investigation of ASU's hiring practices, and continued protesting until, in 1975, the university agreed to negotiate with the students, faculty, and staff.[34]

Chicano Movement activists did not limit themselves to supporting working-class struggles. They also actively organized workers and their families. Of particular importance was the effort to organize undocumented workers to fight for their right to be in the United States. The defense of undocumented immigrants had been ongoing since the early 1900s.[35] Despite this significant history of organizing and defending the most vulnerable in the Mexican-origin community, Chicano Movement activists, as the historian Jimmy Patino noted in his book *Raza Sí, Migra No*, were not initially concerned with Mexican immigration or with the plight of undocumented Mexican immigrant workers in the late 1960s. Some activists were ambivalent about or dismissive of this issue. Others, such as César Chávez and LULAC, opposed the presence of undocumented workers and sought their removal from the country. By the early 1970s, however, activists became more sensitive to the plight of undocumented workers and the issue of immigrant rights.[36]

Three key organizations responsible for centering undocumented immigration issues within the Chicano Movement were Hermandad Mexicana Nacional, CASA, and Committee on Chicano Rights (CCR). Hermandad and CASA were founded by Bert Corona, a longtime labor and community activist in California, with a few other individuals. Corona established Hermandad in the late 1960s to organize undocumented immigrants facing the threat of deportation by the Immigration and Naturalization Service or the Border Patrol and to protect their rights in the detention and deportation processes. In the late 1960s, the Immigration and Naturalization Service and the Border Patrol began to raid jobsites, neighborhoods, and public areas in search of undocumented immigrants. In 1968 Corona decided to organize the undocumented population in order to protect and defend their interests. Hermandad, staffed by volunteers, most of whom were undocumented, not only counseled immigrants on their rights and assisted them in finding housing, but also filed lawsuits charging federal officials with violating immigrants' rights. Because of its services and advocacy, increasing numbers of immigrants joined Hermandad. By 1973 it had chapters in several southern California cities and a few other parts of the country.[37]

In 1968, Corona also established CASA. Like Hermandad, CASA served undocumented immigrants, but it had more legal resident and citizen volunteers on its staff. Mexican American professionals, social workers, priests, pastors, nuns, and students staffed CASA chapters in the early 1970s. CASA provided social services to immigrant workers and their families, opposed state and federal restrictionist immigration policies, and defended the right of undocumented immigrants to work in the United States without fear of being deported.[38] Although it began in Los Angeles, CASA grew into a statewide and regional organization. In 1973, however, it was taken over by what Corona calls "Young Turks," or idealistic and younger activists. These activists transformed the organization from a populist association to one centered around a vanguard group of revolutionary leaders whose goal was to replace the existing capitalist system with a socialist one. CASA did not survive beyond 1978.[39]

A final organization responsible for centering immigration issues in the Chicano Movement was the CCR. Herman Baca, a local activist from National City, California, a small town adjacent to San Diego, established the CCR to advocate for the rights of Mexican immigrants and Mexican Americans. The group demanded an end to violence against Mexican-origin individuals perpetrated by the Border Patrol, police forces, and other state officials. It also called for the abolition of the Border Patrol and the Immigration and Naturalization Service. In contrast to most Chicano Movement organizations, the CCR called for Mexican immigrants (documented and undocumented) and Mexican Americans to work together to end the abuses they faced in this country.[40]

Hermandad, CASA, and CCR all advocated for undocumented workers, educated the public about the importance of the immigration issue to the community, and promoted policies aimed at defending immigrants' rights. Because of their activism as well as the significant increase in undocumented Mexican immigration and growing public opposition to it, the plight of this group of workers became a central concern of the Chicano Movement by the mid-1970s.

Chicano intellectuals also acknowledged the working-class nature of the Mexican-origin community in their academic studies. Chicano studies historians, and scholars more generally, began to research the living conditions of Mexican-origin workers, their resistance to exploitation throughout the nineteenth and twentieth centuries, and the way male and female Mexican-origin workers shaped the American economy. Chicana and Chicano labor history became one of the most important fields of study during the 1970s.[41]


## Race

A second major focus of the Chicano Movement was race. Struggles against racism and racial discrimination in American society were widespread during the 1960s and 1970s. Chicano activists, inspired by different ideologies and perspectives, established a large number of organizations throughout the country and fought against personal and institutional forms of racism in American society.

They tackled institutionalized racism in foreign policy, law enforcement, and the administration of justice. Activists, for instance, opposed the war in Vietnam, police brutality, and inhumane treatment in prisons. The largest action of these years was the growing opposition to the war in Vietnam, fueled by the increasing numbers of Mexican Americans who were dying in another country. Many people viewed the war as racist and as being fought primarily by Americans of color. In opposition to the war, Mexican Americans formed local and state "moratorium" committees and organized antiwar rallies.[42] A national rally against the war in Vietnam was held on August 29, 1970, in Los Angeles, California. This protest, the largest by any minority group, was attended by more than twenty thousand individuals. Its goals were to force the federal government to end the war in Vietnam and bring American troops home. Unfortunately, the police disrupted the rally, killing four Mexican American activists, including the nationally syndicated columnist Ruben Salazar.[43] This and several other repressive police actions effectively destroyed the Mexican American opposition to the war in Vietnam.[44]

Chicano activists also opposed racial discrimination in the electoral system, the public schools, and higher education. Those opposed to the two-party system established the independent Raza Unida Party to fight for control of important policy-making institutions. La Raza Unida Party was initially discussed at a conference sponsored by Reies Tijerina in 1967, then officially inaugurated in 1970 in Crystal City, Texas. Raza Unida chapters quickly developed throughout the U.S. Southwest and

Midwest. A national Raza Unida Party convention took place in 1972, but instead of building unity it only led to further divisions between two major leaders of the Chicano Movement—José Ángel Gutiérrez from Texas and Corky Gonzales from Colorado.[45]

Other activists contested racism in public education. Community organizations and activists challenged the assimilationist curriculum in the elementary and secondary grades and fought for the establishment of ethnic studies, bilingual education, and multicultural education in the public schools. College students and their organizations questioned the exclusion of Mexican American history and culture from college and university curricula and struggled to establish Chicano and Chicana studies courses, departments, and centers in their institutions.[46] Finally, activists, primarily Chicanas, fought against racial and class discrimination in the white feminist movement. Chicana feminists argued that the white feminist movement ignored racism and fought for rights and services that benefited the middle class only.[47]

Some of these struggles lasted for short periods while others continued for years or decades. The movement against the war in Vietnam, for instance, lasted for a handful of years. Chicanas/os began to organize against the war in 1968, but repression in the early 1970s caused a significant decline in protests. The push for Chicana/o studies courses at the university level began in 1968 and continues in the twenty-first century. Since 2010 this struggle has expanded to the high school level.[48]

Because of internal differences and institutional repression, many of these activists were unable to achieve their ultimate goals.[49] Differences between Chicano activists and organizations were common between 1968 and 1978. These differences in many cases led to clashes over how to agitate for specific causes, such as the antiwar moratorium.[50] Sometimes tensions and clashes took place within a single organization, such as MEChA, La Raza Unida Party, CASA, and the Brown Berets.[51]

Clashes between Marxists and cultural nationalists, for instance, were quite frequent within the student movement. Marxists in general sought to gain control of student movement organizations, particularly MEChA, in order to promote their specific agenda of building a revolutionary party or to support a Marxist-sponsored rally or demonstration. In one case in 1973, Marxists criticized the cultural nationalism of

Chicano students at a MEChA state conference. They urged the group to adopt Marxism as the ideology for the organization. MEChA refused to do so. The continuing clash between Marxists and nationalists at the conference disillusioned many apolitical students who were present. It also discouraged many Marxists from continuing their participation in MEChA. The ultimate result of these clashes was the decline of MEChA on college campuses in California.[52]

Clashes between cultural nationalists and feminists over issues of political praxis, leadership, and double standards in sexual relations on college campuses and in the community also undermined the goals of Chicano Movement activists throughout the country. Unlike Marxists, feminists did not seek to control the movement or redirect it to serve their own agendas. Instead, they sought to strengthen the movement by allowing women to participate as equal partners in the struggles for social justice and by seriously addressing their issues and concerns.[53]

The clash between feminists and cultural nationalists is best represented in the events that took place within the California State, Long Beach, chapter of MEChA between 1968 and 1973. There, Chicano MEChA members asked some Chicana members to help recruit and politicize incoming Chicana students in order to increase the membership and clout of the organization on campus. For two years, Chicanas worked feverishly to increase the consciousness of Chicana students enrolling at the university and to encourage them to join MEChA. During that time, however, the men treated the women with disrespect and ignored some of the emerging issues they were facing. One major issue was the growing numbers of Chicanas dropping out of college, especially due to pregnancy.[54] As tensions increased, feminists soon formed their own group—Las Hijas de Cuauhtémoc—and their own press in order to continue their work in the Chicano Movement.[55]

Divisions and clashes were also frequent between nationalist activists in Chicano Movement organizations. A clash of this type took place at the national Raza Unida convention in El Paso in 1972. Two leaders— Corky Gonzales and José Ángel Gutiérrez—battled for national leadership of La Raza Unida Party. They had competing visions of nationalism, different motivations for assuming this position, different goals for the party, and diverging ideas on the strategies and tactics needed to

move forward. Their unwillingness to compromise left the party fragmented and weak and prevented the formation of an effective national
structure.[56]

Governmental surveillance and state repression likewise played
important roles. They disrupted many ongoing struggles against racism and discrimination in American life and undermined the Chicano
Movement.[57]

## *Gender*

Another major focus of the Chicano Movement was the development of
a feminist praxis. By a feminist praxis I mean that the political involvement of women was imbued with a feminist consciousness and guided
by the need to confront or eliminate the reality of patriarchy as a system of oppression within the Chicano community and in society in
general. In practical terms, this meant that Chicanas themselves began
to deal seriously with their own concerns and issues in these struggles. Although criticized by cultural nationalists for their feminist ideas,
Chicana activists worked alongside their male counterparts to challenge racism and discrimination against the Mexican-origin community. They actively and extensively involved themselves in the Chicano
Movement and helped establish a slew of organizations from the UFW
to La Raza Unida Party to the Mexican-American Education Council
(MAEC).[58] They also were members in and worked to maintain long-
standing organizations such as LULAC and PASSO.

Chicana feminists engaged with a variety of issues. They organized
marches, pickets, and demonstrations; recruited members to Chicano
Movement organizations; made speeches about the issues of discrimination, exploitation, and degradation; protested the war in Vietnam;
defended the community against law enforcement abuses; conducted
research on immigrants, and lobbied against anti-immigrant legislation.[59] They both assumed leadership of student, youth, or community
organizations and worked with existing groups to improve educational
opportunities for students from kindergarten to university. As members
of these organizations, they strengthened the historic struggle against
racial, class, and gender discrimination in the United States.

Chicanas had diverse experiences in male-dominated Chicano Movement organizations. Originally, Chicanas were members of UMAS and MEChA who informally provided political education to recruit young Chicanas into the organization, but their involvement became a mechanism for voicing complaints about the contradictions within these organizations and about male sexism. They challenged the dismissive attitudes of male leaders, the sexual politics of the movement, the gendered division of labor, and discrimination against the only Chicana leader of MEChA from men who were threatened by her leadership. Anna NietoGomez served as vice president of the California State University, Long Beach, chapter of MEChA in 1968–69 and as president in 1969–70. The men held meetings behind her back, tried to silence her by hanging her in effigy, and rejected being represented by a Chicana at the statewide MEChA meetings.[60]

Regardless, women continued to articulate their issues and concerns, and to advocate for an explicitly Chicana gendered political identity. Men decisively rejected their political vision and called their ideas divisive. They also called Chicana activists derogatory names, such as sellouts, *vendidas*, or Malinches (all meaning traitors). Male responses to Chicana feminists, as Maylei Blackwell notes, suggest that nationalism was not merely an ideology of cultural pride but a gendered construction of political involvement.[61] Still, Chicanas in MEChA were not deterred. They continued to organize independently of men, forming Las Hijas de Cuauhtémoc. They also established a newspaper to voice their concerns and needs, founded the first Chicano Movement–era feminist journal, *Encuentro Femenil*, and began formulating early Chicana feminist thought.[62]

Chicanas also participated extensively but painfully in other movement organizations. In the UFW, for instance, women like Dolores Huerta and Helen Chávez worked alongside men to negotiate union contracts, to support union efforts to improve working conditions and salaries for farmworkers, and to manage the daily operations and funding of the UFW. In most cases their participation was undervalued and unappreciated.[63] Chicanas involved in organizations such as CASA and the East Los Angeles chapter of the Brown Berets devoted themselves to the movement despite their objections to sexism from their male colleagues. CASA did not recognize Chicanas' identity as feminists due to its Marxist ideology. Marxism cast women's issues as an equal part of the class struggle not as a separate movement for equality. The reality, however, was that women continued to experience sexism, sexual politics, and gendered division of labor. Nevertheless, they worked for the success of CASA and were profoundly influenced by it; even after it folded, Chicanas continued their activism in other organizations and struggles.[64] Chicanas involved in the East Los Angeles chapter of the Brown Berets had a quite distinct experience from the women in CASA. Initially, women participated as equals in the Brown Beret chapter, but over time they became segregated and were treated as subordinates. They first protested this gender inequality, then large numbers eventually left the group and organized on their own to foster their collective identity as feminists.[65]

Women also played key roles in La Raza Unida Party in Texas and in the MAEC, a grassroots organization in Houston. Women demanded or were encouraged to participate in the organization's activities and to assume leadership roles. For instance, women played key roles in the formation and development of La Raza Unida Party. Although the party remained male dominated, Chicanas helped build its structure, develop its platform, and assume leadership positions at the state, county, and local levels.[66] In Houston, women were also encouraged to participate in the founding of MAEC. Throughout the two-year campaign for legal equality, Chicanas were actively involved in MAEC decision-making and in the implementation of these decisions. Even in cases where males led, women in Houston still played a key role in shaping MAEC's development. Local MAEC activist Celine Ramírez, for instance, noted that while their husbands were the leaders, "the men rarely were by themselves, they were usually with their wives." Furthermore, the men did not make any major decisions without their wives' input and did not take any actions unless the women agreed. Abe Ramírez and Mario Quiñones, two prominent leaders of MAEC, agreed with her assessment. "We wouldn't do anything without them," stated Ramírez.[67] Some of these activists even argued that men led only because women allowed them to do so. Celine Ramírez argued that the men, especially those who were married, could not do anything, including assume leadership positions, unless they got their wives' approval.[68]

Chicana activists not only helped to strengthen the historic struggle against racial discrimination in American life, they also expanded it to include issues and concerns they faced as women.[69] At times feminists struggled against specific acts of gender discrimination. One example was the fight to stop the coerced sterilization of Mexican-origin women at the Los Angeles County–USC Medical Center during the 1960s and 1970s. Many of these women spoke no English and were tricked or forced to have tubal ligations without their permission or while under duress, such as during the late stages of active labor and as they awaited emergency cesarean sections. Once Mexican Americans heard about this injustice, a group of mothers, young Chicano lawyers, and activists worked with the doctor who blew the whistle to expose the sexism and racism of hospital administrators and to halt these practices.[70] Community activists eventually filed a lawsuit, *Madrigal v. Quilligan*, against hospital administrators. Antonia Hernández led the argument in the courts on behalf of the Mexican-origin women. Although they lost the case in 1975, activists continued their campaign against hospital abuse in the public arena and the state legislature. Between 1975 and 1979, their persistence led to new state guidelines requiring medical practitioners to obtain educated consent from candidates for sterilization and to the repeal of a 1909 law that permitted eugenic sterilization. Furthermore, the activism against sterilization abuse contributed to the development of a discourse on reproductive rights that challenged the prevailing understanding of reproductive freedom as being limited to abortion and birth control.[71]

Feminists, generally speaking, mobilized against sexist, racist, classist, and uncaring policies enacted by federal, state, or local agencies. For instance, they fought for prison reform, welfare reform, cultural awareness, better services for working-class women, and more integration and visibility of women in religious and social institutions. They also tackled a variety of issues dealing with education, reproductive rights (birth control, abortion, pregnancy, and health-care services), and bilingual radio services.[72] Chicana feminists, in other words, worked by themselves, with men, and with other women of color in different sites of struggle to contest the racist, sexist, and homophobic policies of local, state, and national leaders and to create a world devoid of these multiple oppressions.[73]

Finally, feminists contributed to the establishment of Chicana studies as a field of study. As early as 1971, Chicana feminists called for the inclusion of their concerns in Chicano studies departments and in the emerging scholarship on the Chicano community. They also called for the development of Chicana courses in Chicano studies programs and in the university in general. Chicanas likewise contributed to the reassessment of important female historical actors and influenced the development of history and other academic fields of study.[74]

## Culture

A final focus of the Chicano Movement pertained to culture. Nationalism encouraged activists to reject assimilation and to both defend and show pride in their history, culture, and language. Activists pursued two major strategies in their quest for cultural affirmation. One focused on opposing the devaluation, suppression, or repression of the Spanish language and Mexican culture in mainstream institutions, especially the public schools. Chicano high school students were instrumental in challenging the oppressive institutional practices aimed at preventing the use of Spanish in the public schools. This became one of the key demands in practically all the high school walkouts conducted during the late 1960s and early 1970s.[75] Still others protested negative stereotypes of Mexicans in popular culture, education, and the media.[76]

As reparation to undo the damage to their heritage, activists demanded that mainstream institutions use, acknowledge, and respect their language and culture. They demanded culturally based reforms of American institutions. In education, for instance, they demanded bilingual and bicultural instruction, ethnic studies, and multicultural education. Others simply called for "culturally relevant" education, or learning that incorporated the language and culture of Mexican American students.[77]

Another strategy was cultural reclamation. Most activists sought to reclaim and educate people about their rich cultural heritage. They

reaffirmed their pride in Mexican culture and either began to study it
or to participate in its promotion and creation. Large numbers of young
people in the public schools, universities, and neighborhoods, for example, joined folklórico dance troupes or mariachi and conjunto music
groups. Some went to Mexico to study the origins of folklórico while
others formed musical groups that played traditional Mexican songs.
Still others used their artistic, musical, or writing skills to produce
plays, visual art, poetry, or prose that reflected their experiences in the
United States or that supported the goals of the Chicano Movement.[78]
Chicanos and Chicanas across the country, for instance, established
*teatro* groups, produced movies reflecting their perspectives, painted
murals on all types of surfaces, and formed artist collectives.[79] They
also established a Chicano literature based on new themes and forms
of expression.[80]

The growing nationalism and activism of the community also influenced Chicano musicians and the music they played. *El movimiento*
had a significant but differential impact on Chicano music in California versus Texas. Some groups, for instance, changed their name and
image to reflect the ethnic consciousness of the Chicano Movement.
One example is the California group El Chicano, which originally
went by the name of The VIPs. Like many teenaged groups during
the early 1960s they wore matching outfits, were clean-cut, and performed rhythm-and-blues music with English lyrics that had nothing
to do with activism, ethnic pride, or barrio conditions. With the rise of
the Chicano and counterculture movements in the United States, the
band changed its name to El Chicano, abandoned the matching outfits,
grew long hair, and performed songs that incorporated Latin rhythms,
instruments, or lyrics.[81] Musicians also founded new groups with Spanish names. Some of the most popular new groups in California were
Santana, Malo, Azteca, Sapo, and Tierra. In Texas, new groups that
reflected the ethnic pride of the Chicano Movement included Ruben
Ramos and the Mexican Revolution as well as Latin Breed.

Many musicians responded to the ferment in the community by
composing, rearranging, performing, or recording songs that supported
el movimiento or that reflected some of its themes. Some musicians
appropriated existing songs and translated them into Spanish; others

composed or arranged songs in support of Chicano Movement struggles. Two songs that supported farmworkers were "De colores" and "No
nos moverán." The first spoke about the objective of uniting people
of all colors in support of farmworkers, and the second to the determination of farmworkers not to be moved from their primary goal of
unionization and economic justice.

Other songs contained lyrics that reflected the songwriters' growing
pride in their Mexican heritage or that addressed a variety of Chicano
economic and political concerns.[82] One of the most popular songs composed during these years was "Yo soy chicano," a tribute to the growing numbers of individuals in the Mexican American community who
took pride in viewing themselves as Chicanos.[83] Songs like "Don't Put
Me Down If I'm Brown," by El Chicano, or "Chicanita," by the Royal
Jesters, spoke to the growing pride and desire for respect in the Chicano community. Chicano musicians likewise responded to the brown
power movement by becoming more ethnic, but in different ways. California musicians Latinized the American music they were performing;
Texas performers switched from playing a mixture of American and
Mexican music to playing mostly the latter.[84] Although Mexican American musical styles in California and Texas were differentially affected
by the Chicano Movement and the social ferment swirling around it,
musicians continued the tradition of combining American and Mexican
music to create something new for those growing up during the 1960s
and 1970s.

The Chicano Movement, in sum, was a complex and multifaceted series
of explorations guided by multiple ideological strands of nationalism.
The many ideological strands woven into the movement led to a variety
of tension-filled and conflictual episodes. Although thousands of individuals participated in countless struggles, the movement had four major
foci during its most important years from 1968 to 1978. Activists struggled against class exploitation, racial discrimination, sexism, and cultural
suppression. While the Chicano Movement per se vanished from the
public eye after the 1970s, many of the struggles initiated during this
important period continue to this day. In other words, el movimiento did
not disappear, it evolved.

## CHAPTER 4

# Moderates and the Struggles against Racism and Discrimination, 1969–1978

During the years of radicalism, Mexican American moderates did not disappear. Rather, they continued and expanded their activism. Many of these activists were continuing their work in organizations such as LULAC, AGIF, MAPA, and PASSO. But a new generation of moderate leaders also emerged during the Chicano Movement years. These leaders believed in some of the key ideas of the Chicano Movement, including the need for self-determination, pride in Mexican cultural heritage, and widespread community involvement, but they did not embrace separatism, direct action tactics, or confrontation. In the early years of the Chicano Movement, some Mexican American activists did utilize what one historian called "measured militancy," the combined use of lobbying, advocacy, and occasional direct action tactics to achieve moderate change.[1] By the early 1970s, however, many of these individuals had abandoned militant methods and become more accommodating in how they pursued their goals.[2]

This new generation of moderate leaders emerged out of the struggles of the Chicano Movement and formed such organizations as MALDEF, the East Los Angeles Community Union (TELACU), SVREP, the Congressional Hispanic Caucus, PADRES, Las Hermanas, and many others to build on the efforts of earlier activists. Moderate Mexican American activists were as much a part of the Chicano Movement as were the radicals. The major difference was that moderates continued to believe in the liberal agenda, conventional methods of struggle, gradualism, and working with established political leaders to combat their primary concerns of discrimination and poverty.

Moderates continued to be involved in civil rights activities during the Chicano Movement years. In many cases, the young moderates worked with the older generation to promote social and economic justice. In a few cases, groups of long-established moderates worked on their own through venues such as LULAC and AGIF to challenge the unfair treatment of their community. On other occasions, moderates worked with radicals or took advantage of radical actions to gain concessions from political leaders.[3] As in the past, moderates tackled a variety of issues and utilized different strategies to achieve their goals.

## DRIVE FOR ELECTORAL EQUITY

One key issue addressed by moderates during the Chicano Movement years dealt with voting rights and representation in the electoral arena. Mexican Americans had been involved in local and state elections for decades. In the 1960s they increased their participation at the national level and played a crucial role in presidential politics. Although this was a significant step in the political development of the community, they still faced significant barriers to full participation, especially in local and state elections. While more radical members of the community sought to take control of local and state governments through the creation of a new political party, La Raza Unida, others sought to increase the participation of all Mexican Americans in the political process by promoting voter education, registration, and involvement. One of the individuals who participated in this moderate approach was Willie Velásquez.

As a young man in the mid-1960s Velásquez helped found MAYO and La Raza Unida, but he soon abandoned radical politics for a more moderate approach aimed at increasing the community's participation in elections. In the early 1970s he established SVREP, which became one of the most important organizations at the forefront of major social and political gains for the U.S. Latino community.[4] It was fundamental in promoting and encouraging Mexican American participation in elections at all levels and in increasing the number of Latina and Latino officeholders.

To this day, the mission of SVREP, founded in San Antonio in 1974, is to empower Mexican American and other minorities by increasing their involvement in the electoral process. The organization conducted research on political issues in the community and developed programs to organize and mobilize voters around an agenda that reflected their values. The motto it adopted reflected these ideals: "Su Voto Es Su Voz" (Your Vote Is Your Voice). SVREP engaged in several key activities during the 1970s and 1980s. First, it expanded nationwide to register and educate voters, and promote voting in upcoming elections. Second, it worked alone or with other initiatives on get-out-the-vote drives. Third, it advocated at the local, state, and national levels to raise awareness and support voting rights issues.[5]

Another organization that played a key role in Mexican American empowerment was MALDEF. Started in San Antonio, it quickly grew into a national organization. Its purpose was to protect and promote the civil rights of Latinas and Latinos in the United States in the areas of employment, education, immigrant rights, and political access. MALDEF engaged in several types of activities. First, it filed lawsuits to fight for the rights of immigrants and citizens from Latin America. Second, it advocated for and educated the community about civil rights concerns. Third, it worked with other civil rights groups to oppose policies and practices that infringed on the rights of all Latinos and Latinas in the country.[6]

MALDEF's initial efforts during the late 1960s and early 1970s were chaotic and directed at school segregation, police brutality, and denial of due process to Chicano Movement activists. During these years it embraced radical causes and both sympathized with and supported radical leaders. From 1973 to 1984 MALDEF shifted its focus to other areas, particularly increasing Mexican American access to political power in the Southwest.[7] During the 1970s and early 1980s MALDEF played a key role in the growing political empowerment of the Mexican American community.

Under the new leadership of Vilma Martínez, MALDEF significantly increased access to voting rights in Texas. Martínez was born in San Antonio in 1943. Like many Mexican Americans, she grew up in a poor neighborhood and faced many gender and racial barriers. She however was quite determined to overcome all obstacles that came her way, graduating from high school with honors. She went on to earn a law degree from Columbia University in 1967.[8] For several years she worked as a civil rights lawyer for the National Association for the Advancement of Colored People Legal Defense and Education Fund and as a labor lawyer for a prestigious law firm in New York City. In 1973, she became MALDEF's general counsel and its third president.[9] Martínez expanded the group's funding sources, initiated leadership training for Latina and Latino elected officials, and tackled voting rights issues.

Joaquín Ávila, a staff attorney, led the voting rights efforts for MALDEF. Born in Los Angeles in 1948, he grew up in Compton, California. On graduating from Harvard Law School in 1973, he joined MALDEF. He once stated that he did not become a practicing lawyer to make money but to "effect social change.[10]

In 1974, Ávila teamed up with Willie Velásquez from SVREP to battle voting inequities. Between 1974 and 1984 MALDEF and SVREP jointly filed eighty-eight voting rights lawsuits. Ávila litigated many of these cases by arguing that at-large election structures diluted minority voting strength.[11] Velásquez, known for his fiery speeches, generally followed up with community voter registration drives. One lawsuit argued by Ávila, for instance, challenged San Antonio's at-large election system. Its success was one of the major factors contributing to the establishment of a single-member-district voting system, which eventually led to the election of Henry Cisneros as a city councilman in the late 1970s and then as mayor in the 1980s.[12] These developments significantly increased voter registration in the community.

MALDEF also worked with other civil rights groups to support federal voting rights legislation that would benefit non-English-speaking minorities at the state and local levels. In 1975, they successfully lobbied for amendments to the Voting Rights Act (VRA) of 1965 that extended the law's provisions to non-English-language minority groups and enacted a bilingual election requirement. This provision required election officials in jurisdictions with large numbers of non-English speakers to provide ballots and voting information in the language of these constituents. The bilingual election requirements were controversial, with proponents arguing that bilingual assistance was necessary to enable recently naturalized citizens to vote and opponents arguing that they constituted costly, unfunded mandates.[13]

After the adoption of the VRA of 1975, MALDEF and other civil rights groups joined the federal government to sue hundreds of county commissions, city councils, and school boards to force them to adopt voting structures that provided Mexican Americans greater access to elected positions.[14] A major result of these federal and local actions was an increase in the number of Mexican Americans elected to office. For example, within a decade and due to the persistent efforts of organizations such as SVREP and MALDEF, the number of Mexican Americans holding state, county, and municipal offices in the Southwest increased. In Texas, the increase was significant. In 1973, there were 565 Latina/o elected officials in the state. By 1984, the number had grown to 1,427. The vast majority of these individuals were Mexican Americans.[15]

California, Arizona, Colorado, and other states saw similar increases in Latina and Latino elected officials. Change was also apparent at the national level. The number of Latino representatives in Congress, for instance, increased from one in 1960 to six by 1977. Four of these individuals—all Mexican Americans—were elected during the 1960s: Henry B. González from San Antonio (1961), Edward R. Roybal from California (1963), Eligio "Kika" de la Garza II from South Texas (1965), and Manuel Luján Jr. from New Mexico (1969). Luján was a Republican, the others were Democrats.[16] Two Puerto Ricans were elected to Congress in the following decade: Herman Badillo from New York City (1971), and Baltasar Corrada del Río, Resident Commissioner of Puerto Rico (1977).[17] As the number of elected officials increased, so did the variety of new organizations serving the needs of Mexican American and Latina/o legislators. Among these institutions were the Congressional Hispanic Caucus and the National Association of Latino Elected Officials at the national level, the Mexican American Democrats and the Mexican American Legislative Caucus in Texas, and the Chicano Legislative Caucus (later the Hispanic Legislative Caucus) in California. Mexican American representation in political office continued to increase in the following decades, largely due to the federal law and community activism.[18]

## NATIONAL APPOINTMENTS

During the late 1960s and the 1970s, politically moderate Mexican American activists also continued their quest for representation in the federal government. Since the early 1960s, LULAC, AGIF, and other groups had been pressuring the president to appoint Mexican Americans to high positions in the federal government. At times a host of new moderate Mexican American organizations, such as the Southwest Council de la Raza (later named National Council de la Raza), used their limited resources to advocate for such appointments.

The push to name Mexican Americans to important agencies, commissions, or committees at all levels of government began with the election of John F. Kennedy as president in 1960. The calls became more strident once President Johnson assumed the presidency in 1963. Despite this pressure the president did not make any significant appointments until the latter part of his administration, when he appointed Vicente Ximenes as head of the EEOC and as chair of the Inter-Agency Committee on Mexican-American Affairs. Over the next several months, Johnson established a variety of federal agencies, commissions, and advisory committees and appointed Mexican Americans to direct or lead them. Among the more visible appointments were those of Henry M. Ramírez, Armando M. Rodríguez, and Lupe Anguiano (see chapter 1).

Johnson continued to appoint Mexican Americans to important positions in the federal government during 1968. According to the Inter-Agency Committee on Mexican-American Affairs, at least 131 Mexican Americans and Puerto Ricans were appointed to or hired into mid-level and upper-level positions in the federal government or judiciary, including the Advisory Committee on Mexican American Affairs, the Commission on Civil Rights, and district courts in Puerto Rico. Some of the individuals Johnson appointed to important positions were Benigno C. Hernández, ambassador to Paraguay; Raúl H. Castro, ambassador to Bolivia; Raymond Telles, chair of the U.S. Section, United States–Mexico Commission for Border Development and Friendship; Admiral Horacio Rivero Jr., Commander in Chief, Allied Forces, Southern Europe; and Julián Samora, chair, National Advisory Committee on Income Maintenance Programs.[19]

The pressure for continued appointments to important positions in the federal bureaucracy continued under President Richard M. Nixon, a Republican. Like Johnson, Nixon created new agencies, committees, and commissions and appointed "Spanish-speaking Americans" to them during the late 1960s and early 1970s. One of Nixon's primary interests was support of small businesses, especially minority-owned businesses. As president he focused on promoting black and brown capitalism. In 1969, soon after getting elected, Nixon hired Hilario Sandoval, a Mexican American businessman from El Paso, to head the Small Business Administration (SBA). Sandoval and two others—Martín Castillo, a federal bureaucrat, and Ben Fernández, a financial consultant—organized the National Economic Development Association (NEDA) to encourage the development of Latina and Latino businesses. Funded by the SBA and the Department of Commerce, NEDA fostered countless Latina/o businesses in more than thirty urban areas. Although NEDA did assist in the development of some businesses, critics in the barrios of the Southwest felt that it did little to promote brown capitalism. Ruben Salazar, a prominent *Los Angeles Times* reporter, claimed that Mexican Americans in the barrios started calling NEDA "NADA" (nothing), because it played no meaningful role in economic development.[20]

Nixon also created the Office of Minority Business Enterprises in 1969, made a large number of federal appointments, and supported the Inter-Agency Committee on Mexican-American Affairs. He renamed this office the Cabinet Committee on Opportunities for Spanish-Speaking Affairs (COSSA) in 1971 and appointed Dr. Henry M. Ramírez to continue the tradition of using this office to increase the Latina and Latino presence in the federal government and in American life in general.[21] In August 1971, Nixon showed up at the first COSSA meeting and ordered a nationwide recruitment drive to appoint and hire "Spanish Americans" for executive decision-making positions. He directed department heads to open top jobs for Mexican Americans, Puerto Ricans, and Cubans in all divisions of the executive branch. The campaign was implemented by Counselor Robert Finch and headed by Ramírez. President Nixon's order led to several more appointments. According to a January 7, 1972, report, he had made twenty-six presidential appointments and appointed seven Spanish-surnamed persons as regional directors of federal agencies.[22] By the end of the year, fifty-four Spanish Americans had been appointed to important positions.[23]

President Nixon also made a number of appointments to federal boards, commissions, and advisory committees. Among some of the individuals he appointed were Carlos Villareal to head the Urban Mass Transportation Administration; Ray Telles as EEOC commissioner; Louis Núñez as deputy staff director of the U.S. Commission on Civil Rights; Bert Gallegos as general counsel and Phillip Sánchez as director of the Office of Economic Opportunity; Carlos Conde as White House staff assistant; Antonio Rodríguez as consultant to the White House; Rudy Montejano as commissioner of the Interstate Commerce Commission; and Romana Acosta Bañuelos as U.S. treasurer.[24]

Despite these improvements, Ramírez, director of COSSA, felt that the progress was too slow and encouraged all agency heads to strengthen their efforts. During the next year and a half, taskforces were established in eleven departments to "study, define, and formulate action plans with set schedules" for the appointment or hiring of Latinas and Latinos.[25] For many agency heads, the establishment of affirmative action committees in their areas was an unwelcome development. Only a few engaged seriously in this process. One of the few that did was the Office of the Attorney General in the Civil Rights Division, headed by J. Stanley Pottinger. Although he devoted a great deal of time and effort to hire Mexican American lawyers, few high-level appointments were made. Still, the vigorous attempt by Ramírez and his staff to implement the president's August 1971 order led to a gradual increase in the number of Latinas and Latinos appointed to or hired by the federal government.[26]

The Mexican American push for high-level appointments continued for the rest of the decade. Because of their lobbying, President Gerald Ford, Nixon's successor, made more than twenty high-level appointments, one of which was Fernando De Baca as special assistant for Hispanic Affairs. In the late 1970s, Jimmy Carter appointed about two hundred Mexican Americans and Hispanics to high-level positions. Among the most important were Ralph Guzmán to the Department of State and three ambassadors: Raúl Castro to Argentina, Julian Nava to Mexico, and Mari-Luci Jaramillo to Honduras.[27] By the end of the decade, however, the historian Rudy Acuña critiqued these appointees as being responsive not to the Mexican American community but to those who appointed them to office.[28]

## CONTESTING RACISM AND INSTITUTIONAL DISCRIMINATION

In addition to promoting the election or appointment of Mexican American officeholders, the activism of Mexican American moderates encompassed a host of activities aimed at contesting racial discrimination and mistreatment of Mexican Americans in public and private life. As in prior decades, Mexican American activists contested the severe underrepresentation and negative portrayals of their community in mainstream institutions such as the movie and television industry, as well as the negative attitudes expressed by political, social, and judicial leaders. The AGIF, for instance, protested prejudicial comments made by a local judge in California in 1970. In this case the judge referred to Mexican Americans as "lower than animals" and as "miserable, lousy, rotten people." He continued that maybe Hitler was right in getting rid of "the animals in our society." The AGIF mounted organized protests and argued that his comments were a national disgrace for the California judicial system.[29]

In another case, the National Mexican-American Anti-Defamation Committee, the Incorporated Mexican American Government Employees, and the AGIF systematically criticized offensive ethnic stereotypes in the mainstream media. Two of the images they objected to were the Frito Bandito and the José Jiménez character created by the comedian Bill Dana.[30] The Frito Bandito was a cartoon mascot for Fritos corn chips in commercials broadcast beginning in 1967. The Frito Bandito, who spoke broken English with an exaggerated Mexican accent, robbed people of their Fritos corn chips and complained that he was being pursued by the "Frito Bureau of Investigation."[31] These ads perpetuated the "Mexican bandit" stereotype that had been portrayed in Hollywood Westerns since the 1920s. Frito-Lay eventually retired the Frito Bandito character in 1971. José Jiménez was a Mexican character who likewise spoke with a heavy accent in broken English. Although U.S.

comedian Bill Dana and other Americans thought the character's linguistic shortcomings were humorous, the José Jiménez character offended many individuals in the Mexican American and Latina/Latino community. The criticisms and protests had little influence on the comedian, but he later retired the character.[32]

Meanwhile, other activists fought for reform in religious institutions. As several scholars have noted, religion has had a profound influence on Mexican American culture and activism for hundreds of years.[33] During the years of the Chicano Movement, both radical and moderate advocates sought changes in how Catholic and Protestant houses of worship related to the Mexican American community. Radicals, for the most part, protested the church's neglect of the community's material needs.[34] In contrast, moderate activists negotiated with or lobbied, pressured, and petitioned church officials to become more sensitive to the dire needs of poor Mexican American communities. The Catholic Church came under especially critical scrutiny. During the years of radicalism, moderate activists pressured the church to appoint Mexican Americans to higher ranks of the clergy, devote more resources to poor communities, and become more involved in solving the problems of their parishioners.

Two organizations that promoted change within the Catholic Church without resorting to confrontation were Padres Asociados para los Derechos Religiosos, Educativos, y Sociales (PADRES) and Las Hermanas. The former was founded in San Antonio, Texas, in 1969 by several diocesan priests who included Ralph Ruiz, Henry Casso, Franciscan Manuel Martínez, and Jesuit Edmundo Rodrigues.[35] Its purpose was to apply pressure on the Catholic Church hierarchy to appoint Mexican Americans as bishops and Spanish-speaking priests as pastors in Spanish-speaking communities. Other objectives were to advocate for greater attention to the material needs of the poor and working classes, for establishment of a Mexican American unit of the National Liturgical Commission to adapt the liturgy to Mexican American culture, and for church support of the UFW grape boycott.[36]

PADRES petitioned the National Conference of Catholic Bishops to increase the presence of Mexican Americans in the hierarchy. Local priests also petitioned their regional leaders. New Mexican priests succeeded in getting Roberto Sánchez formally appointed archbishop of Santa Fe in July 1974. Sánchez strengthened the Hispanic ministry and developed a variety of cultural preservation programs during the 1970s and 1980s. He also was the first bishop to offer an apology to the local Native American communities for the history of mistreatment initiated by the Spaniards in the late 1500s. Although loved by the people of the archdiocese and respected by his fellow bishops, Sánchez resigned in 1993 after charges of sexual assault were filed against him. He died in 2012 at the age of seventy-seven.[37] In Texas, Mexican American priests lobbied to have Patricio Flores named as auxiliary bishop for San Antonio in May 1970. Flores, the first Hispanic bishop in the nation, had been one of the founders of PADRES and was one of the group's most outspoken members. He was a strong supporter of the farmworkers' movement in California and Texas and of Mexican American civil rights. He, like others in the city, showed great pride in his Mexican culture and heritage.[38]

Las Hermanas, founded in 1970 in Houston by Sisters Gloria Gallardo and Gregoria Ortega, was a national organization of Latina Catholic women. It began as an organization of religious women, but its membership soon expanded to include all Catholic Hispanic women. The goals of the organization were to increase the Catholic Church's awareness of the needs of the community, to work for social change, to train Catholic women to be community leaders, and to exert pressure on the Catholic hierarchy toward these ends. Unlike PADRES, which ceased to exist as an organization by the 1980s, Las Hermanas continued to be active into the early twenty-first century. It succeeded in getting religious women more actively involved in meeting the social needs of local communities, supporting the UFW grape boycott, and organizing conferences on regional issues affecting women.[39]

Politically moderate Mexican American activists also targeted a variety of Protestant churches. Mexican Americans in the Mennonite Church, for instance, played instrumental roles in negotiating with church leaders to become more accepting of Mexican Americans and other minorities; to deal more directly with issues of discrimination against women and racism confronting Mexican Americans, Puerto

Ricans, African Americans, and Latinas in the church; and to support the farmworker movement in California.[40]

During the Chicano Movement years, moderates, at times in collaboration with radicals, protested a large number of other discriminatory policies and practices in employment, health care, law enforcement, and immigration. The AGIF and LULAC, for instance, battled employment discrimination in private industry and in the federal government, especially the lack of Mexican Americans in the U.S. Postal Service. In one case, the AGIF mounted a decade-long struggle against Coors Brewing Company for failing to hire Mexican Americans into executive positions.[41]

Other Mexican American activists protested the coerced sterilization of poor Latina women at a southern California hospital, the killing and abuse of Mexican Americans by police, and harsh immigration policies, especially those proposed by Congress and by the Carter administration in the mid-1970s.[42] Mexican American moderates likewise tackled educational inequities and initiated significant efforts to reduce discrimination and improve the instructional opportunities of Mexican American children. This topic will be covered in chapter 5.

Moderate groups, unlike their radical counterparts, for the most part did not organize rallies against discriminatory institutional policies and practices. When radicals called for direct action tactics, moderates often participated in them. However, they preferred to lobby, negotiate, or dialogue with elected officials or policymakers to reach amicable decisions and develop policies they could support.

## FROM GRASSROOTS ORGANIZATIONS TO COMMUNITY DEVELOPMENT CORPORATIONS

Finally, moderates engaged in significant grassroots community development. Some activists expanded their efforts or initiated new ones to revitalize and improve their communities by developing affordable housing, establishing community-based businesses, providing social and educational services, and promoting cultural activities. One of these groups was LULAC.

By the early 1970s LULAC chapters were not as prominent as they had been in prior decades. Many of them were inactive while others tended to focus on social rather than civil rights activities. Although preoccupied with settling debts incurred by LULAC president Joseph R. Benites in 1973 and 1974, LULAC devoted its resources to program development for the rest of the decade. For instance, it initiated a variety of affordable housing projects. Having sponsored its first two government-funded housing projects in the early 1960s, LULAC expanded this activity during the 1970s. In a span of eleven years, from 1962 to 1973, LULAC sponsored eight housing projects worth close to $18 million. Three of these projects were located in San Antonio, three in Corpus Christi, and one each in El Paso and Kingsville, Texas.[43]

LULAC also collaborated with AGIF, the Department of the Navy, and the Department of Labor to develop the largest national job training and placement program in the country, known as Operation SER. Operation SER began in the mid-1960s as a small program that provided job training and placement assistance for low-skilled Mexican American workers in Corpus Christi, Texas. By 1979 LULAC and the AGIF had 130 Operation SER programs in ninety-eight cities across the nation. This program successfully placed thousands of Mexican Americans in new jobs and helped them to improve their lives.[44]

In the mid-1970s, LULAC established two major programs aimed at raising corporate funds for the organization and at improving the educational status of Mexican American students in secondary and postsecondary institutions. One of these was the LULAC Foundation, created in 1974. Corporate funding enabled LULAC to settle its debts and expand its activities. The other was the LULAC National Educational Service Centers (LNESC), created in 1973. With the creation of LNESC, LULAC centralized its educational effort into a network of sixteen counseling centers coordinated by an office in Washington, DC. Its mission was to increase educational opportunities for Hispanic students through the development and implementation of effective programs in local communities around the country. These centers provided thousands of students each year with educational counseling, scholarships, mentorships, leadership development, and literacy programs.[45]

Joining LULAC were new local organizations that began as part of the Chicano Movement and soon transformed into community development corporations (CDC). A CDC, funded by the federal government, was a nonprofit entity established by local community leaders to improve the social and economic well-being of a specific geographical area designated as a "special impact area." To accomplish its goals, a CDC operated for-profit businesses designed to make money for the nonprofit corporation so that it could fund the provision of social services and reduce poverty.[46] These organizations helped revitalize local communities by economically and politically empowering residents.

Six major Mexican American CDCs were formed in the Southwest during the late 1960s and early 1970s: TELACU in California; Chicanos por La Causa (CPLC) in Phoenix, Arizona; the Mexican American Unity Council (MAUC) in San Antonio; Siete del Norte in New Mexico; the Spanish Speaking Unity Council in Oakland, California; and the Denver Community Development Corporation in Colorado.[47] Although each corporation had a distinct origin, all were influenced by federal legislation on CDCs. These corporations played significant roles in empowering local communities in the Southwest and channeling much-needed resources to help reduce poverty, improve material conditions, and promote cultural pride. The histories of the six CDCs illustrate the crucial roles they played in enhancing power and pride in their respective communities.

TELACU, the most successful of the CDCs in the Southwest, was founded in 1968 by labor activists and community leaders interested in combating the high levels of poverty and unemployment faced by poor and disadvantaged communities in East Los Angeles. The initial committee, developed by the United Auto Workers, was led by Esteban Torres, a local community leader. The committee, fueled by ideas of self-determination derived from Chicano Movement ideology and aided by federal War on Poverty funds, eventually became TELACU. This group developed a comprehensive approach to community development in the East Los Angeles area that included establishment of affordable housing, creation of community business enterprises, provision of educational and job training opportunities, and sponsorship of cultural development projects.[48] Although it was plagued by scandals in the early 1980s, TELACU continued to prosper. Through its successful investments in real estate, banking, construction, and a variety of other businesses, it was able to provide jobs to hundreds of local residents and to assist with the housing and mental health needs of low-income individuals, especially seniors, immigrants, and youth. Its political clout also increased as a result of the election of Mexican Americans to local, state, and national positions.[49]

CPLC began in 1969 as a Chicano Movement organization of college student and community militants, but by the following year it transformed into a CDC. The group's initial actions focused on political and educational issues; for example, CPLC fielded a slate of candidates for local school board elections. Although its members did not win election, this was the first electoral experience for many activists who eventually became what the historian F. Arturo Rosales has called the current "core of Chicano political leadership in Maricopa County, Arizona."[50] CPLC also organized walkouts at Phoenix Union High School to protest the lack of Mexican American courses and teachers, inadequate school funding, racial tension between blacks and Mexican Americans, and racial discrimination.[51] Although it initially engaged in radical activities, once it became a CDC, CPLC moderated its confrontational style and began to focus on building affordable housing, developing social services like job training and counseling, promoting economic development in the community, and preserving its rich cultural and historical heritage.[52]

MAUC was founded in 1967 by Albert Peña Jr., Mario Compeán, Juan Patlán, and Willie Velásquez. By the 1970s, it had abandoned its confrontational style and transformed from a grassroots militant organization into a CDC. MAUC became active in three major aspects of community improvement in the San Antonio barrio: affordable housing, educational and social services, and economic development.[53]

Other activists developed faith-based grassroots organizations to pressure local officials to improve their neighborhoods by ensuring accountability, channeling resources to the community, and increasing civic involvement. The best-known group of this type was Communities Organized for Public Service (COPS). Ernesto Cortés Jr. played a key role in its formation. Cortés was born and raised in San Antonio, Texas. Like many Mexican Americans in that city, he grew up on the poor side of town and experienced contempt and discrimination from Anglo-Americans. During the radical years of the Chicano Movement, Cortés, who was then a college student, organized a statewide support group for the UFW. From 1969 to 1972, he served as deputy director in charge of economic development and housing for MAUC in San Antonio. During those years he also trained under Saul Alinsky, a legendary community organizer and founder of the Industrial Areas Foundation (IAF). Cortés joined the IAF in 1972.[54]

The IAF, a group dedicated to grassroots community organizing, was established by Saul Alinsky in Chicago during the 1930s. Entities established by the IAF worked on a large number of local issues and developed structures through which ordinary citizens could "effectively negotiate with the government and private institutions that affect[ed] their lives."[55] The IAF had a track record of supporting Mexican American organizations. In the 1950s, for example, it supported the formation of the CSO.[56] The CSO chapter in San José, California, served as an organizational tool for a young César Chávez, who later established the UFW, one of the key organizations of the Chicano Movement. The IAF continued to support Mexican American organizational development during and after the Chicano Movement years, including the founding of COPS and Metro Alliance in San Antonio, and the Valley Interfaith Project in Phoenix.[57]

In 1974, a young Cortés returned to San Antonio and used his IAF training to form COPS. This church-based grassroots group was composed of twenty-six parishes in the predominantly Latino, low-income West Side and South Side of the city.[58] Its members were profoundly religious and deeply attached to their families and local communities. This faith served as the glue that guided the organization through the decades.[59] For the next several years, COPS mobilized Mexican Americans in San Antonio to lobby public officials for the needed resources to improve material conditions in the barrio and to increase the community's educational and employment opportunities.[60] Initially confrontational in its approach, over the years COPS modified its tactics and began to deal with local leaders in a less aggressive manner.

The first major action taken by COPS illustrated its early militant outlook. In August 1974 about five hundred members of COPS attended a San Antonio City Council meeting and demanded to be heard. Two individuals—Father Albert Benavides and Beatrice Gallego—confronted Mayor Charles Becker and the city council. They accused the city officials of diverting city funds from the inner city to newly developed subdivisions on the North Side of town. As a journalist noted several decades later, an angry Benavides and a forceful Gallego charged city officials with "stealing from the poor West and South side neighborhoods to provide funds for developers in the affluent North Side suburbs." The city funds being diverted were earmarked to be spent on projects in the West Side such as much-needed storm sewers.[61] Father Benavides told the mayor and city council that these projects had been authorized for decades but never completed. His powerful presentation and the presence of hundreds of community activists forced city officials to restore these funds to their intended purposes. "It's possible," noted Moises Sandoval, an observer of local developments, "that if COPS had not intervened then, the West Side might still be waiting for the drainage projects today."[62]

COPS continued its involvement in civic affairs and community development for the next several decades. In the 1980s, it joined forces with other community-based organizations to politically and socially empower poor and lower-middle-class Mexican Americans and African Americans in San Antonio.[63] Its involvement in local affairs transformed the city's social and political order. It helped shatter the city's established conservative structure by transforming the way in which officials were elected, increasing the representation of Mexican Americans on the city council and the school board, redirecting millions of dollars in government funds to improve conditions in the West and South Sides of San Antonio, establishing important job training and educational programs benefiting Mexican Americans, and keeping politicians accountable and honest. "For the past 30 years," noted one commentator, "COPS has been the conscience of the San Antonio and Bexar County electoral system. Through their civic vigilance, and rigorous accountability sessions, COPS has steadfastly worked to keep politicians honest, fair, and accountable to the voters."[64]

Secular community-based grassroots organizations were also active during the radical Chicano Movement years. Like their faith-based counterparts, these alliances fought for better housing, for neighborhood preservation, and against the destruction of their communities. In Phoenix, Arizona, the CPLC engaged in community efforts to preserve the Golden Gate Barrio in South Phoenix. Its efforts failed and local leaders razed the neighborhood to build a new airport.[65] In El Paso, Texas, Mexican American residents of El Segundo Barrio mobilized and initiated multiple efforts to protect the residential and cultural character of their neighborhood. They deployed three means of activism to fight local leaders: grassroots neighborhood political organizations, squatter demonstrations, and community-based cultural preservation projects. Unlike the CPLC in Arizona, the residents in South El Paso successfully challenged the urbanizing visions of city leaders and politically empowered themselves in the process.[66]

Mexican American moderates—that is, those who believed in working for change within the political system and opposed direct action tactics—responded in various ways to the radicalism swirling around them but continued their own agenda of gradual social reform. While some moderates criticized the radical agenda and its politics, others were sympathetic to the goals and actions of Chicano Movement activists. The majority however were more concerned about their own moderate path of social, economic, and educational reform. Moderate leaders continued and expanded the struggle for equality and equity that had begun in the early twentieth century. A new generation of activists fought against discrimination in the electoral arena and began efforts to increase community empowerment by promoting voter education and participation in local, county, state, and national elections. Long-standing organizations like the AGIF and LULAC, and recent ones like MALDEF, mounted campaigns against demeaning media stereotypes and racist individuals in mainstream institutions, against discrimination in federal employment and in private industry, and for a variety of programs that would meet the social and educational needs of the Hispanic population. Moderates, in other words, continued to pursue the historic liberal agenda of reform while radicals protested in the streets and demanded dramatic social change. Of particular importance within the moderate camp was the emergence of a movement to reform the public schools that educated masses of Mexican American students around the country. Advocacy for quality education became an important component of the renewed campaign for equality in American society. The final chapter focuses on these activists.

# Moderates and the Quest for Educational Equality during the Years of Radicalism

During the Chicano Movement years, moderate activists continued to be involved in the struggle for civil rights and educational equity without resorting to confrontation or protests. Because the popular press concentrated on radical activity, moderates' efforts remained largely unnoticed, unreported, and unknown. Like other moderates during this period, educational activists took a variety of actions against institutionalized racism and used multiple strategies to promote educational opportunities. These activists contested discrimination in education, advocated for special programs to support Mexican American schoolchildren, and became agents of change from within the public schools.

## ANTI-DISCRIMINATION STRUGGLES

As in earlier decades, discrimination in public education remained widespread in the 1960s and 1970s, and educational equity for Mexican American students remained a prominent concern. Some activists directed their efforts at the local or state levels, while others concentrated on promoting changes at the federal level. Those working at the local level—primarily parents, union members, and grassroots agitators—had faith in mainstream institutions, especially the courts, and filed lawsuits against various forms of discrimination. As in earlier decades, Mexican Americans mounted legal challenges to school segregation in many parts of the Southwest. More than thirty such lawsuits were filed during these years.[1]

Moreover, parents and community activists also filed lawsuits against unequal school quality, the exclusion of immigrants from public education, biased testing, and subtractive English-only policies.[2] Although it was lawyers who argued these cases, working-class parents and community activists were instrumental in ensuring their success. One such parent was Demetrio Rodríguez, lead plaintiff in *San Antonio v. Rodríguez*, which challenged the unequal financing of public schools. In the 1960s Rodríguez was a sheet metal worker employed at a local air force base in San Antonio. As a veteran who had served in World War II and the Korean War, Rodríguez was involved in local struggles for equality as a member of both AGIF and LULAC. Like other parents in the Edgewood School District, he knew little about school funding, but he was familiar with the segregated, inferior, and financially strapped public schools in the district. Together, he and the other parents raised questions about their schools and why the system seemed unfair. Why did inequality exist, they wanted to know, and what could be done about it? Believing that the courts could make just rulings that would equalize the schools, the parents filed one of the most important lawsuits of the late 1960s and 1970s.[3]

Moderates at the national level—who were mostly federal bureaucrats, agency appointees, and consultants—also combated school discrimination. During the late 1960s and early 1970s, an increasing number of them were appointed to important positions in select federal agencies such as the Office for Civil Rights (OCR) and the Department of Education. Others were appointed to national advisory committees on education or to committees within federal educational agencies. In these positions, they contributed to the shaping of federal policies that addressed exclusionary and discriminatory practices in local schools. Mexican American activists played key roles in at least two major educational policies during the 1970s: the May 25, 1970, Memorandum and the Lau Remedies of 1975. The active participation of Mexican American activists in the implementation of the May 25, 1970, Memorandum offers insight into the ways in which they contributed to fighting local school discrimination at the national level.

## THE MAY 25, 1970, MEMORANDUM
## AND MEXICAN AMERICANS

In 1970 the OCR, an agency of HEW, issued the first major federal response to the issue of discrimination against Mexican Americans and other national-origin minority children in the country.[4] This memo, dated May 25, 1970, directed that Title VI of the Civil Rights Act of 1964 must be applied to Mexican Americans. Title VI prohibits discrimination on the basis of national origin, color, or religion in any federally sponsored activity.[5]

The memorandum identified four major areas of concern that local school districts had to address in order to comply with Title VI. The first addressed the exclusion of national-origin children from effective participation in a school district's educational program due to "inability to speak and understand the English language." It stipulated that the district had to take "affirmative steps to rectify the language deficiency in order to open its instructional program to these students."[6] The second issue involved assigning national-origin minority children to special education classes or denying them access to college-preparatory courses on the basis of their English language skills.[7] The third limited the use of ability grouping or tracking in the schools based on these children's special language needs. It stipulated that any such system "must be designed to meet such language skill needs as soon as possible and must not operate as an educational dead-end or permanent track." Finally, the memo stipulated that in order for school communications with these children's parents to be adequate, "such notice may have to be provided in a language other than English."[8]

Furthermore, the memo directed local school districts to examine their current practices "in order to assess compliance with the matters set forth in this memorandum." If a district believed that it was not in compliance, it was to contact the OCR immediately and outline what specific steps were being taken to remedy the problems. If the district needed help in developing a remediation plan, OCR would provide technical assistance and "any additional information that may be needed to assist districts in achieving compliance with the law and equal educational opportunity for children."[9]

Soon after the memo was issued, OCR began to develop procedures for identifying and remedying noncompliance. Three major tasks were necessary: (1) developing a process for investigating school districts for compliance; (2) establishing an educational assistance capability to help districts come into compliance, and (3) developing additional policies aimed at specific discriminatory practices in each area of the memo.[10] Mexican Americans played key roles in all of these tasks.

In May 1970, J. Stanley Pottinger, the director of the OCR, established a taskforce to develop policies for each topic in the memorandum and to assist in their implementation.[11] The chair of the group was Martin H. Gerry, special assistant to the director, and members came from both inside and outside the department. Significant numbers of Mexican American bureaucrats, educators, psychologists, and both community and civil rights leaders were invited to participate.[12] During the latter part of June the OCR task group held a conference in Denver, Colorado, to discuss its responsibilities and to determine priorities for policy development.[13] This conference, argues James V. Gambone, represented "the first official inclusion of national origin leaders at a high level of government policy-making."[14]

The group decided to focus on the first part of the second section of the memo, dealing with the assignment of national-origin-minority-group children to classes for students with mental retardation. After reviewing and discussing the factors contributing to these assignments, the group reached its conclusion. The OCR had to take action to adequately identify the various discriminatory aspects of the assignment process and identify an alternative, nondiscriminatory system of assignment for use by school districts found to be out of compliance.[15] Consequently, the group decided to appoint a committee to develop and present a draft policy for enforcing the appropriate assignment of students to special education classrooms. While targeting discriminatory placement of Mexican American children into special education classes, the group also made several policy suggestions pertaining to many other forms of discrimination that national-origin-minority-group children experienced in their schools.[16] The taskforce drafted comprehensive recommendations and sent them to Pottinger who, in turn, forwarded them to the secretary of HEW.[17]

Over the next several months, the committee charged with drafting a policy on assignment to special education met in different locations. On November 18, 1970, it delivered a draft of its deliberations to a task group meeting in San Diego, California. Three months later, on February 4, 1971, the task group met in San Antonio to study the recommendations further. While in the city, the members visited Edgewood Independent School District in West San Antonio, the fourth poorest school district in Texas. More than 96 percent of the students in the district were nonwhite, and most of them were Mexican Americans. Two years previously, the district had hired Dr. José A. Cárdenas as superintendent. He and a management team composed of Gloria Zamora, Teresa Dent, and Blandina "Bambi" Cárdenas had implemented significant school innovations aimed at improving the district's financial status and the academic achievement of Mexican American students.

Under Cárdenas's leadership, the school district had doubled its budget and had introduced a host of instructional reforms.[18] These reforms were based on the theory of incompatibilities, developed by José Cárdenas and Blandina Cárdenas (no relation). This theory provided evidence that school districts with large populations of Mexican American children in poverty could implement comprehensive and effective changes if "they were tied to a comprehensive analysis of how school district processes impact children as well as the innovative programs designed to respond to them."[19] The task group team was impressed with the ongoing changes and expressed interest in incorporating some of these ideas into their deliberations. As members discussed the actions needed to ensure that national-origin-minority-group children would not experience discrimination in assignment to special education classes, Pottinger reported they dealt "with those basic components of a nondiscriminatory assignment mechanism which was compatible with sound EMR [educationally mentally retarded] practices and complied with Title VI of the Civil Rights Act of 1964."[20]

The following month the Office of Education, at Pottinger's request, established the Intra-departmental Advisory Committee on Bilingual Education to develop strategies for identifying and developing programmatic responses to the May 25 Memorandum. This committee also was charged with supervising and assisting school districts found to be in noncompliance with the instructional program and parental notification requirements.[21] Forty-one members were on this committee, of whom twenty-five were Mexican Americans and at least three were Puerto Ricans. Martin H. Gerry cochaired the committee with Gilbert J. Chávez, director of the Office for the Spanish-Speaking in the Office of Education. Most of these individuals were actively involved in bilingual education advocacy or administration.[22] The advisory committee invited seventy-five Mexican American, Puerto Rican, and Native American educators to meet in San Diego from April 28 to 30, 1971, to develop bilingual/bicultural program models for the Office of Education. The conference was divided into five groups, each addressing a specific topic: program of instruction, bilingual/bicultural materials, parent policy groups, teacher training, and evaluation designs. The groundwork was also laid for the selection of professional educational teams to be sent to school districts interested in developing compliance plans under the May 25, 1970, Memorandum.[23] The committee invited several scholars and officials involved in the design and implementation of bilingual/bicultural education to present recommendations for the OCR compliance plans. Among them were Dolores Earles, Juan Aragón, Manuel Ramírez, and José A. Cárdenas.

Earles described the bilingual/bicultural educational programs in the Laredo (Texas) United Consolidated Independent School District.[24] These programs were designed to ensure that Spanish-speaking children had equal access to the educational program. Aragón presented the rationale for a culturally responsive staff development plan congruent with the memorandum.[25] Ramírez outlined the Follow Through model in Rancho Cucamonga, California. This model revolved around a rigorous program of bilingual education aimed at promoting significant institutional change.[26] Cárdenas focused on the Edgewood model, the most recently developed approach, based on the Theory of Incompatibilities developed by Blandina Cárdenas and José A. Cárdenas. This theory posited that the problem of underachievement was complex and necessitated a comprehensive solution. Schools could not develop a specific programmatic response to one problem at a time in isolation from other problems. This would be a dysfunctional response to the interrelated set of incompatibilities. As Blandina Cárdenas wrote, "It is necessary, therefore, that rational modifications of the educational program be responsive to most or all of the incompatibilities."[27]

The participants at the conference endorsed the Edgewood model and corresponding theory of incompatibilities. At the end of the meeting they recommended a comprehensive approach to school change that would comply with the May 25 Memorandum provisions.[28] The Cárdenases' approach to school reform resonated through recommendations in the following months. On June 4, 1971, a subcommittee of the advisory group on bilingual education met in Long Beach, California, to develop specific recommendations for OCR. By then all the members agreed that OCR should advance a comprehensive educational plan rather than supplementary programs. A follow-up meeting in Boston, Massachusetts, the following week reaffirmed that a comprehensive approach to school change was needed.[29]

Both as committee members and as experts on school reform, Mexican Americans also helped develop an educational assistance capability in OCR.[30] Over the next two years, OCR conducted pilot studies in the Beeville, Del Rio, and El Paso school districts in Texas to assess the appropriateness of their procedures for defining compliance versus noncompliance with the May 25 Memorandum. Moderate Mexican American educators, whether members of the taskforce, OCR program staff, or participants in advisory committees and other groups, played key roles in these efforts.[31]

## ADVOCATING FOR SPECIAL PROGRAMS

While significant numbers of moderate activists were contesting educational discrimination at multiple levels of government, others were advocating for special programs targeted to the cultural, linguistic, and academic needs of Spanish-speaking children. In the early 1960s, there was no consensus on which programs would effectively boost academic achievement. In light of the diversity of needs, Mexican American educators and their allies supported a variety of special programs, including compensatory, migrant, and early childhood education.[32] By the end of the decade, however, consensus began to coalesce around bilingual education.

Although bilingual education was not clearly defined in these years, all the existing programs in the Southwest addressed the linguistic needs of Spanish-speaking children as one component of their educational plan. The limited data on Mexican American schoolchildren indicated that their academic achievement was low and they dropped out in large numbers. According to one report, approximately 80 percent dropped out of school before graduation.[33]

In the early to mid-1960s, linguists, educators, and foreign language teachers advocated for the use of Spanish with a gradual introduction of English as a solution to the problem of low achievement and high dropout rates among Mexican American students. Others emphasized the need to bridge the cultural differences between Mexican-origin students and the Anglo-American-oriented curriculum.[34] Ignoring the students' cultural heritage, many educators argued, diminished their self-esteem and cultural identity and contributed to the problem of school leaving.[35] They hoped bilingual education would address these linguistic and cultural concerns, as well as other problems, including the exclusion of the Mexican American community from the schools and the inflexibility of school practices.[36] Educators and community activists, then, supported bilingual education for several reasons. First, it increased academic achievement. Second, it maintained the language and culture of Mexican children while they learned English and American ways. Third, it reinserted the Mexican American community in their children's education. Finally, it reduced discriminatory and ineffective school practices.[37]

Growing support for bilingual education, favorable political factors, and Mexican American lobbying gradually led to the enactment of language policies at all levels of government during the late 1960s and early 1970s. The U.S. Congress passed the first bilingual education bill in late 1967 and President Johnson signed it in early 1968. Its passage encouraged state legislatures and local decision-making bodies to enact their own bilingual education legislation and policies during the next several years.[38]

During the 1960s and 1970s, Mexican Americans were actively involved at every stage of bilingual policy development and at every level of government. These elected officials, federal bureaucrats, educators, and community activists did not engage in confrontation or direct action tactics like the radical activists. They turned to lobbying, negotiation, and compromise in their quest for bilingual educational programs in public schools serving Mexican American students. They played different roles in bilingual education policy development at various levels of government. Some, like María Urquides, helped establish the national intellectual and political foundations of bilingual education. Urquides attended the public schools in Tucson, Arizona, graduating from high school in the mid-1920s. Urquides taught in a segregated Mexican American school from 1928 to 1949, then in a predominantly Anglo-American school from 1948 to 1955.[39]

In 1955, she was recruited to teach at Pueblo High School, where the student body was about 70 percent Mexican American. At Pueblo, she noticed that Spanish-speaking students were having difficulty with reading and writing assignments. They also were reticent about their heritage and tried to Anglicize their names so that teachers could pronounce them. She told these students that they had beautiful names and should be proud of them. She also encouraged them to insist on being called by their given names. "When we mispronounce the Anglo names and say 'Esmeeth' instead of 'Smith,'" she would remind them, "they correct us and make us repeat it until we pronounce it correctly. So why can't we do the same thing?"[40]

She promptly met with Adalberto Guerrero, Henry "Hank" Oyama, Rosita Cota, and other teachers to discuss the problems students were having in school and propose solutions. In 1958 they decided to apply for federal funds under the newly signed National Defense Education Act. Enacted as part of the space race after the Sputnik incident in 1957, this act provided funds for the teaching of math, science, and foreign languages.[41] Over the next several years, she took the lead in promoting the benefits of practicing bilingualism in the classroom and encouraged political leaders and legislators to formulate, enact, and implement bilingual education programs at the national, state, and local levels.[42]

Other Mexican Americans played key roles in either crafting these bills or lobbying legislators to vote for them. Lupe Anguiano and Armando Rodríguez, for instance, consulted on the drafting of the first federal bilingual education bill, which U.S. Senator Ralph Yarborough introduced in 1967.[43] Anguiano was a farmworker-activist working for the Office of Education. Rodríguez was the head of the newly established Mexican American Unit in the Office of Education.[44]

Edward Roybal, a Democrat from California, also played a key role in the passage of this bill. Roybal had a long history of fighting for the rights of national minorities, immigrants, and workers. Continuing his fight for the rights of Mexican American public school students, in 1967 he sponsored the bill in the House of Representatives, worked with influential members of Congress, and lobbied additional representatives to vote for it.[45] Mexican American state legislators, teachers, administrators, school board members, parents, businesspeople, scholars, and community activists also advocated for this bill as citizens and worked with legislators to ensure its passage. At least eleven of the twenty-two activists playing crucial roles in the passage of the Bilingual Education Act of 1967, were Mexican American:

> Braulio Alonso, public school administrator in Tampa, Florida, and president of the National Education Association (NEA) (1967–1968)
>
> Lupe Anguiano, War on Poverty project administrator in Los Angeles, California, and staff member, Mexican-American Affairs Unit within the Office of Education
>
> Joe Bernal (D), state senator from Texas
>
> José A. Cárdenas, chair, Department of Education, St. Mary's University, San Antonio, Texas, and director, Mexican American Education, Southwest Educational Development Laboratory, Austin, Texas
>
> Father Henry J. Casso, vicar of urban affairs, San Antonio, Texas
>
> Adalberto Guerrero, professor of romance languages, University of Arizona, Tucson, and director of the Arizona chapter of the NEA
>
> Edward V. Moreno, foreign language consultant, Ventura, California, and president of the California Association of Mexican-American Educators

Albar Peña, assistant professor of education, University of Texas
   at San Antonio
Robert Reveles, administrative assistant to Congressman Morris
   Udall (D-AZ)
Armando Rodríguez, director, inter-group relations, Califor-
   nia State Department of Education and chief, Mexican-
   American Affairs Unit, Office of Education
María Urquides, dean, Pueblo High School, Tucson, Arizona,
   and director, Arizona chapter of the NEA

Others contributed to enacting or strengthening bilingual education
policies at the state and local levels. Two key individuals in the Texas
legislature were Representative Carlos Truan from Corpus Christi and
Senator Joe Bernal from San Antonio. Bernal had supported many progressive causes during his tenure in the state legislature. After attending a crucial bilingual education conference in Tucson, Arizona, in
1966, he became convinced that bilingual education could improve
academic achievement among Mexican American students in Texas and
the country overall.[46] He supported the national movement for bilingual education and spearheaded the effort in Texas after 1967.[47] Truan,
a junior legislator elected to office in 1968, took over as leader of the
bilingual education movement in Texas after Bernal lost his bid for reelection in 1974.[48]

   These supporters of bilingual bills at the federal and state levels
participated in traditional acts of civic involvement and political per-
suasion, not radical action. They conducted research on the problems
confronting Mexican American children in the public schools; lobbied
for bilingual legislation at local, state, and national gatherings; testified
before Congress; and advocated for bilingual education with other legislators and key political leaders.

## CHANGE AGENTS FROM WITHIN

While some moderate activists filed lawsuits against discrimination
or engaged in advocacy, others became agents of change from within

public education. In the late 1960s and the 1970s, increasing numbers of Mexican Americans were elected to local school boards and hired as superintendents, administrators, teachers, and support staff in the public schools. In these positions, many of them took it upon themselves to fight from within the school system for the rights of Mexican American children and for educational equity. They set out to replace exclusionary, discriminatory, assimilationist, and demeaning policies, programs, and structures with equitable, inclusive, pluralistic, and caring alternatives that fostered children's learning.

Many of these individuals were in the trenches of public school reform. Rather than simply studying or criticizing public schools; they actively worked to improve them. Mexican American agents of school change created academic programs, developed innovative curricula, hired and trained staff to work in the schools, provided instruction to students, garnered parental and community support for education, and evaluated the success of these efforts.

Hundreds of school change agents emerged during the Chicano Movement. The activities of these educators are largely unknown. Here I provide profiles of five change agents from Texas, Arizona, and California who became national experts and spokespeople for Mexican American students in the 1960s and 1970s. I hope this discussion begins the process of acknowledging and documenting individual experiences in the campaign for educational equality and equity during the years of radicalism.

The first was María Urquides, a leader of the bilingual education movement in Arizona and nationally. She began her career as a teacher in the late 1920s, then became actively involved in promoting educational change as a teacher at Pueblo High School in the 1950s. At Pueblo she developed new approaches for addressing the low academic achievement of Mexican American students. Instead of complying with the English-only state law on the books for decades, she and her colleagues—Adalberto Guerrero, Henry "Hank" Oyama, and Rosita Cota—focused on providing instruction that supported students' learning. They also found ways to acknowledge rather than stamp out their Mexican cultural identity.[49]

With federal funds provided by the newly enacted National Defense Education Act, Urquides and her colleagues developed a more linguistically and culturally responsive curriculum. They decided to begin by instructing Mexican-origin children in Spanish. These children already spoke Spanish, but most of them could not read or write in their native language. Consequently, they developed a "Spanish for Spanish-Speakers" class that would promote literacy. They also redesigned the curriculum because, as Adalberto Guerrero noted, their students could not identify with the materials that presented only Spanish culture. Using their federal funds, they developed a curriculum that portrayed the history, culture, and art of both Mexico and Spain. Although listed as foreign language courses, this curriculum was designed to improve Spanish speakers' academic achievement. The curriculum celebrating the history, culture, and art of Mexico as well as Europe served to counteract the subtractive model of Americanization that governed the educational experiences of Mexican American students in the public schools.[50]

The idea of reintroducing non-Anglo language and culture into the school was radical because of the dominance of English-only pedagogy and forced assimilation. From the early 1900s, speaking languages other than English had been prohibited in the schools. Many school districts with large numbers of Spanish speakers also established no-Spanish rules to reinforce their English-only policies. Under these practices, Mexican American children were punished for speaking Spanish not only in the classroom, but also in the halls and in outdoor activities.[51] Additionally, if not omitted and erased from the curriculum, the heritage of Mexican-origin children was demeaned and devalued.[52]

The teaching of linguistically and culturally responsive classes began in 1959. The offerings became extremely popular over the years and soon had significant enrollments. By the early 1960s these classes began to improve the students' academic achievement and ethnic identity. Pueblo High soon received recognition for its innovative Spanish-language instruction and culturally relevant curriculum. In 1965, the school received the Pacemaker Award for "leading the way" in secondary education. This was the highest honor that the NEA, the largest educator group in the country, gave to public schools.[53] This award and Urquides's continuing involvement in both school reform and civic and educational groups earned her a reputation as an educational expert. Because of her experience in promoting school success among Mexican American students, she became an effective advocate for the establishment of bilingual education programs nationwide by the mid-1960s.[54]

Henry M. Ramírez was another pioneer of successful school reform. The eldest of six children, he was born and raised in southern California during the early years of the Depression. His parents had crossed the border from Mexico into the United States in search of better opportunities in 1924. After several years, they finally settled in the barrios of Pomona. Ramírez earned a BA and teaching credential from Loyola University in 1957 and began his career as a teacher that year. Eventually, he received a PhD in education from Loyola.[55]

In 1965, while teaching in Whittier, California, Ramírez developed the New Horizons program targeting at-risk Mexican American high school students. With the support of his principal, he developed an innovative and comprehensive program of school change aimed at improving their low academic achievement. He defined five desired outcomes of New Horizons and designed an evaluation plan to collect data on them. He anticipated measurable improvements in average daily attendance, grade point average, reading level, extracurricular participation, and both high school graduation and postsecondary education enrollment. His program encouraged parent participation, modified teacher in-service training at his school, monitored daily attendance, established a remedial program for students reading below grade level, and reviewed a variety of school policies and practices that were detrimental to students' performance. He also founded a student club and took students on a series of fieldtrips to workplaces, businesses, mountains, beaches, and places of historical interest in the area. Steadily, the academic performance of participating students improved and growing numbers of them began to enroll in two-year and four-year institutions of higher learning. By 1966 the New Horizons program was receiving local, state, and national publicity and awards.[56]

Armando Rodríguez was likewise born in Mexico and came to the United States with his family in the 1920s. He spoke no English when he enrolled in the public schools in San Diego, California. He became fluent in English, graduated from high school, and obtained a teaching certificate in 1949. Later in life he obtained a doctorate in education, became involved in electoral politics, and was appointed to several important federal positions, including assistant commissioner of education.

He began his career in 1949 as a special education teacher at Memorial Junior High School in San Diego, the same school he had attended. Although he was not qualified as a special education teacher, the district hired him on an emergency basis until he received his certification.[57] Rodríguez taught fifteen students in grades seven through nine. Most were Mexican Americans. He helped them learn the basics of reading, writing, speaking, and arithmetic through home visits, an innovative exercise program, and a sports program emphasizing tumbling, gymnastics, and wrestling. His success soon led to the establishment of a successful school wrestling club. Having shown he could motivate both special education and mainstream students in his school, Rodríguez was appointed to a new district-level position. He was responsible for at-risk youth in eight schools—two elementary, three junior high, and three high schools. While working to provide equal opportunity for these students, he completed a master's degree in special education and a secondary administration credential. Obtaining this degree and credential from San Diego State University in 1953 opened new possibilities for him in the years to come.[58]

In 1959, he was named vice-principal of Samuel Gompers Junior High School in San Diego, becoming the first Mexican American administrator in the district. He was later promoted to principal. While at Gompers, Rodríguez initiated a variety of instructional changes that increased the success of Mexican American students. He remained at Gompers until 1965, when he was appointed to a state-level administrative position.[59] As a teacher and administrator, Rodríguez had experienced the problems Mexican American students faced and had found successful instructional and administrative responses to them.

Nick E. Garza was born on September 10, 1921, in Monterrey, Mexico, and raised in San Antonio, Texas.[60] As principal of J. T. Brackenridge Elementary School in San Antonio, Garza became involved in school reform efforts at the request of Thomas D. Horn, a professor of education at the University of Texas. In the early 1960s, Horn initiated a research project on language development and reading in Mexican American schoolchildren. The objective of the study was to develop oral proficiency in Spanish, then use it to facilitate the teaching of English as a second language. Research-based lesson plans were provided to the classroom teachers for implementation. Horn identified several schools in the San Antonio Independent School District that were candidates for his study, including Brackenridge Elementary. Nick Garza agreed to have his school participate.

The district-wide project officially began in the fall of 1964 with eighteen classes in five elementary schools. By 1967 it had grown to eighty-five classes in nine schools, with Brackenridge having the most classes. Central administrators, principals, teachers, and students strongly supported the effort. End-of-year evaluations showed that Mexican American children who received bilingual instruction were much more successful than those who did not. As Garza stated in a Senate hearing, Spanish-speaking students "have gained confidence and poise, and, for the very first time, are no longer afraid to take part in their endeavors."[61] For the next several years, Nick Garza continued this successful bilingual instruction program in his school and gave expert testimony to educational policymakers at the local, state, and national levels.

The final practitioner I discuss is José A. Cárdenas, one of the most important school change agents during these years. Born and raised in Laredo, Texas, Cárdenas attended local schools. He became a teacher at age nineteen then moved into administration after earning an EdD from St. Mary's University. By the mid-1960s he was working as a supervisor and director of special educational programs, concentrating on migrant children's education. In 1969, he was hired as the first Mexican American district superintendent in the state of Texas. By that time Cárdenas had come to believe that the schools had failed Mexican American children. The only way to improve the educational opportunities of these children was to initiate comprehensive school reform geared to their diverse needs.

As superintendent of Edgewood Independent School District, the fourth poorest school district out of 1,200 in Texas, he launched an initiative to improve academic achievement among the predominantly Mexican American student population. In a short time Cárdenas, with an energetic management team headed by Blandina Cárdenas, initiated reforms aimed at meeting the cultural, academic, and psychological needs of Mexican American students.

To accomplish his goals, Cárdenas and his management team developed a differentiated instructional program to fit the cultural and learning styles of Mexican American students at elementary and secondary levels. He instituted bilingual education to address the language difficulties of many Spanish-speaking students, early childhood education for kindergarteners, and culturally sensitive programs for migrant children. To address the concerns of many children with learning problems he initiated individually prescribed instruction. He also promoted significant community involvement in the schools and in children's education.[62]

Cárdenas and his management team also initiated new staffing patterns, extensive staff training, a cultural reinforcement program aimed at valuing students' heritage, a coordinated program of social services, a more sensitive special education program, and an evaluation design for determining the effectiveness of these activities. In a short period, dropout and grade retention rates decreased, while scores on achievement tests improved. The Edgewood educational plan, as Cárdenas noted in 1972, served to "recognize the responsibility of the educational agency to provide an instructional program which is compatible with [the children's] culture and learning characteristics."[63]

Cárdenas's knowledge of the Mexican American community and the multitude of problems Mexican American students faced in the schools, as well as his experience in teaching students who were different from mainstream children, prepared him to develop an educational plan that promoted comprehensive school change.[64] His experiences as a teacher, administrator, director, and successful reformer in the schools made him one of the leading educational experts in the country. Community activists, court representatives, and federal agencies, among others, sought his advice on how to ensure the rights of Mexican American schoolchildren and improve their school experience.

These five individuals demonstrate the activism of Mexican American educators. While radicals protested the war in Vietnam, demonstrated in support of Chicano studies programs, and struggled against sexism, these educators and moderates like them quietly filed lawsuits against institutional racism, worked within the bureaucracy for social change, and lobbied elected officials to oppose discriminatory and exclusionary school policies and practices.

# Conclusion

This book focuses on the role Mexican American moderates played during the radical Chicano Movement years. It argues that moderates—that is, activists who continued to believe in the liberal agenda of the early twentieth century and to favor conventional means of social change—were an integral part of the progress occurring during this era. Mexican American moderates trace their origins to the early 1920s and to the activism of civil rights advocates during the years from the 1930s to the early 1960s. The historian Mario T. García has referred to these individuals as members of the Mexican American Generation.[1]

Mexican American Generation activists expanded their involvement to the national level during the early 1960s. Members of organizations such as LULAC, the AGIF, and MAPA fought for recognition, acceptance, and resources at all levels of government, especially the federal level. They sought access to federal offices, pressured federal agencies and Congress to investigate their claims of discrimination, and lobbied for additional resources to improve their local communities. By the latter part of the 1960s, a number of them gained a toehold in appointed and elected positions in the executive, legislative, and judicial branches of the federal government. By working with established political leaders, Mexican Americans finally earned acceptance as important actors in mainstream political and social institutions.

Just as moderates were gaining access to mainstream institutions, a few radical voices began to emerge at the local level. Radicalism was nothing new in the Mexican American activist community. A tradition of radical activism had existed in the community since the 1840s until being suppressed during the 1950s. This tradition resurfaced in the 1960s, just as moderate activists were becoming part of the mainstream.

The Chicano activists of the 1960s, unlike their moderate counterparts in national or state agencies, were not interested in holding government positions or elected offices. Their interest was empowering the community and affirming an identity rooted in mestizaje, Mexican cultural and religious traditions, and the Spanish language.

Chicano activists were quite diverse and adopted a range of approaches to social change. Some like César Chávez and Dolores Huerta sought to unionize farmworkers and adhered to a philosophy of nonviolence and direct-action tactics like economic boycotts, marches, rallies, and fasts to achieve their goals. They also used the Spanish language and Mexican cultural and religious symbols to rally Mexicans in their struggles for economic justice. Meanwhile, Reies López Tijerina and his followers turned to violence and armed conflict to fight for the cultural and linguistic rights of former Mexican land grant owners in New Mexico. For him, the struggle was not only about land but also about culture. Corky Gonzales, along with high school and college youth, likewise embraced mass mobilization and nonviolent methods to protest discrimination in American society and the suppression, repression, and erasure of Mexican culture and ethnic identity. Unlike male activists, Francisca Flores and the League of Mexican American Women did not engage in the politics of protest nor did they focus solely on challenging racism in American society. From the very beginning, she and the League resisted both racism and the machismo of male Mexican American activists in the civil rights movement. Under Flores's leadership, the League inspired countless of Chicanas to act independently of men. This diverse cacophony of radical activism during the 1960s largely drowned out the voices and actions of moderate advocates for Mexican American rights.

Radical activists came together and formed the nationwide Chicano Movement by the end of the 1960s. Nationalism served as the glue uniting them and inspiring increasing numbers of other Mexican Americans to join the movement. Because of the diversity of ideas circulating about how to unify the diverse activist sectors of the community, many forms of nationalism emerged and guided the Chicano Movement. Although countless protests were carried out under the banner of nationalism during the 1970s, the Chicano Movement tended to focus on four major concerns: class, race, gender, and culture. The dramatic events and personalities associated with these activists further privileged radical voices and obscured the positive roles that Mexican American moderates were playing during these years.

The Mexican American moderate tradition did not disappear during the Chicano Movement. Rather, it persisted and expanded, often due to the commitment of those involved in long-standing organizations such as LULAC and the AGIF. These organizations continued to fight for recognition, resources, and rights for Mexican Americans during the late 1960s and 1970s. This community of moderate activists cautiously supported the Chicano Movement and selectively worked with radicals to bring about reform. While many of them did not endorse the ideals or tactics of Chicano Movement activists, they nonetheless supported or were influenced by the movimiento.

Hector García and the AGIF, for instance, supported the farmworkers march of 1966 and the struggle for fair wages conducted by the UFW in Texas.[2] Dr. García also supported MAYO students in their protests against the stalling of desegregation orders in Corpus Christi, participating in a sit-in at the superintendent's office in 1972. His support of the students eventually got him arrested.[3] A few key Mexican Americans heading a variety of federal agencies, including Armando M. Rodríguez, the head of the Mexican American Studies Unit in the Office of Education, and Vicente Ximenes, head of the Inter-Agency Committee on Mexican-American Affairs, likewise supported the students who walked out of the public schools in 1968 and the community's struggles against discrimination in education.[4] Finally, members of the AGIF joined other Mexican American activists in supporting the Del Rio rally held in 1969 in support of VISTA workers fired from their positions for opposing Anglo decisions.[5]

LULAC, unlike the AGIF, had a history of rejecting all forms of radicalism. During the 1960s and most of the 1970s, its views of militancy in general and of radical Chicano activity in particular remained unchanged. LULAC decried the aggressiveness and arrogance of Chicano activists and the lawless and radical image they projected. League members were alarmed by the growing nationalistic and separatist aspects of Chicano Movement organizations. They lamented Chicanos' rejection of assimilation, acceptance of socialism and communism, and increasing use of direct action tactics. Radical ideas and behaviors, one LULAC member remarked, were alien to Mexican American history and culture.[6] Although criticized by radical groups for being complacent, opportunistic, and aloof from the concerns of working-class communities, LULAC was proud of its long-standing tradition of fighting for civil rights. LULAC, one of its members claimed, "has done more for our people than all other organizations combined."[7]

By 1979, however, LULAC assumed a more aggressive stance and stood with radicals in opposing government neglect and oppression of Mexican Americans. In other words, by the late 1970s, the Chicano Movement had influenced LULAC and moved it to the left. The election of Rubén Bonilla as LULAC's national president in 1979 demonstrated this dramatic shift. Bonilla was the first LULAC president to meet with the radicals and to use some of their rhetoric in attacking government inaction on Chicana/o concerns.[8]

A few moderates in the Southwest, I might note, were openly hostile to and opposed the radical Chicano Movement. U.S. Representative Henry B. González from San Antonio, Texas, was among the most vocal opponents of the Chicano Movement and its leaders during these years. González was a popular Mexican American elected official with a strong civil rights record. He was elected to the San Antonio city council in the mid-1950s and then to the state legislature in the latter part of the decade. While in office he opposed the passage of several bills aimed at maintaining segregation in the state. In the early 1960s, he was elected to the U.S. Congress and served there until the 1990s.[9]

In the early 1960s, González supported the melon workers in the Rio Grande Valley in their efforts for unionization and a minimum wage. But by the late 1960s, he had become increasingly disillusioned with the growing militancy of Chicano activists. He refused to support the call by County Commissioner Albert A. Peña Jr. to protest the use of Texas rangers as strikebreakers in Rio Grande City. He also opposed MAYO members' discussion of the use of violence to achieve their political goals at a January 1968 gathering. He took no position on the Chicano student walkouts at Sidney Lanier High School in 1968. He also did not support the mass protest over the dismantling of the VISTA volunteer program in Del Rio by the governor and county officials. In fact, he even accused the organizers of the protest of being infiltrated by Cuban communists and of spreading hate in the community. Commissioner Peña, in turn, accused González of selling out to the status quo and of abandoning the Mexican American community.[10]

On April 3, 1968, González attacked MAYO for spreading a message of hate. He also broadened his attack to include agencies funding these militants. He called for an investigation of funding agencies and demanded they quit funding what he called professional spreaders of hate. González's campaign against radical organizations continued for another year and a half. His relentless attacks against what he called communistic and hate-filled speeches by Chicano Movement leaders, especially José Ángel Gutiérrez and Willie Velásquez, scared middle-class moderate and conservative Mexican Americans. Conservative Anglos welcomed these comments.[11]

His continuing attacks on radical leaders had a significant impact on the emerging movement. By 1970, most local community action programs, especially VISTA, had purged themselves of MAYO members, and the Ford Foundation had drastically reduced if not entirely cut off its funding. MALDEF, one of MAYO's strongest supporters and a recipient of Ford Foundation monies, had been persuaded to relocate to California. Other organizations, such as MAUC, chaired by Willie Velásquez, and La Universidad del Barrio, a local alternative college, were pressured to limit their Chicano Movement rhetoric and activities. Finally, elected officials supportive of the radicals, most notably . State Senator Joe Bernal and County Commissioner Peña, lost their reelection bids largely due to González's criticisms of them. Bernal lost his election to González's legislative aide, and Peña to a conservative challenger supported by González.[12]

The majority of moderates, however, were not hostile to radicals and either worked with them or took advantage of radical actions to gain concessions from political leaders. Nonradical activism also expanded as a new generation of moderate leaders emerged out of the Chicano Movement. These activists embraced many of the ideals and goals of the Chicano Movement but not its methods. In the early years of el movimiento some Mexican American activists did engage in "measured militancy," but by the early 1970s, many of them had abandoned these methods and become more accommodating in how they pursued their goals.[13] The new generation of moderates in many cases worked with the older generation to promote social and economic justice. At the same time they supported Chicano Movement activists and worked with many of them to achieve their goals of increased access to rights and resources.

Moderate Mexican Americans were quite active during the late 1960s and 1970s. Despite their activism, the popular, mainstream, and movimiento media ignored, neglected, or marginalized their courageous actions. I argue however that moderate activists, both old-guard and younger ones, were integral to the Chicano Movement. Moderates not only helped sustain the movement during this period, they also engaged in their own battles to expand the struggle for equality initiated by Mexican American Generation activists of the past.

Moderates tackled a variety of issues during these years. For instance, they fought against discrimination in the electoral arena and began efforts to increase community empowerment by promoting voter education and participation in local, county, state, and national elections. Well-established organizations like the AGIF and LULAC and new ones like MALDEF mounted campaigns against demeaning media stereotypes of Mexican Americans and racist individuals in mainstream institutions. They also advocated for a variety of programs to meet the social and educational needs of the Mexican American population. In addition to expanding the campaign against systemic racism and discrimination in American institutional life, they sought to improve the material conditions of Mexican American neighborhoods and worked to empower local communities. Moderate activists, in other words, continued to pursue the established liberal agenda of reform while radicals protested in the streets and demanded abrupt social change. Of particular importance within the moderate camp were educators engaged in reforming public schools that had large populations of Mexican American students. The innovations of those involved in education became an important component of the renewed campaign for equality in American life.

Moderate Mexican American activism, in sum, was quite extensive during the late 1960s and the 1970s. Moderates formed an integral part of the Chicano Movement and advanced many of the same causes as the radicals did. They also were involved in their own struggles for equality that complemented Chicano Movement activism. Their activities reveal that the Chicano Movement was not composed simply of radical students, women, and grassroots activists. The movement also contained moderate activists who believed in the promises of the liberal agenda and the use of conventional tactics to achieve their goals.

# Notes

### INTRODUCTION

1. Mario T. García, *The Chicano Movement: Perspectives from the Twenty-First Century* (New York: Routledge, 2014), 10–15.
2. For a sampling of this literature, see Carlos Muñoz Jr., *Youth, Identity, Power* (New York: Verso, 1990); John Shockley, *Chicano Revolt in a Texas Town* (Notre Dame, IN: University of Notre Dame Press, 1974); Armando Navarro, *The Cristal Experiment: A Chicano Struggle for Community Control* (Madison: University of Wisconsin Press, 1998); Armando Trujillo, *Chicano Empowerment and Bilingual Education: Movimiento Politics in Crystal City, Texas* (New York: Garland, 1998); Armando Navarro, *Mexican American Youth Organization: Avant-Garde of the Chicano Movement in Texas* (Austin: University of Texas Press, 1995); Ignacio M. García, *United We Win: The Rise and Fall of La Raza Unida* (Tucson: University of Arizona Press, 1989); José Ángel Gutiérrez, *The Making of a Chicano Militant: Lessons from Cristal* (Madison: University of Wisconsin Press, 1998); Ernesto B. Vigil, *The Crusade for Justice: Chicano Militancy and the Government's War on Dissent* (Madison: University of Wisconsin Press, 1999); Yolanda Broyles-González, *El Teatro Campesino: Theater in the Chicano Movement* (Austin: University of Texas Press, 1994); Alma M. García, ed., *Chicana Feminist Thought: The Basic Historical Writings* (New York: Routledge, 1997); Lorena Oropeza, *Raza Sí! Guerra No! Chicano Protest and Patriotism during the Viet Nam War Era* (Berkeley: University of California Press, 2005); Ignacio M. García, *Chicanismo: The Forging of a Militant Ethos among Mexican Americans* (Tucson: University of Arizona Press, 1997); George Mariscal, *Brown-Eyed Children of the Sun: Lessons from the Chicano Movement, 1965–1975* (Albuquerque: University of New Mexico Press, 2005); Maylei Blackwell, *Chicana Power: Contested Histories of Feminism in the Chicano Movement* (Austin: University of Texas Press, 2011); García, *Chicano Movement*; Lorena Oropeza, *The King of Adobe: Reies López Tijerina, Lost Prophet of the Chicano Movement* (Chapel Hill: University of North Carolina Press, 2019). Marc Simon Rodríguez has argued that although Chicano Movement leaders were militant and resorted to the politics of protest, their reforms were moderate in nature. See Rodríguez, *Rethinking the Chicano Movement* (New York: Routledge, 2015).

3. García, *Chicanismo*, 8.

4. Mario T. García, *Mexican Americans: Leadership, Ideology, and Identity, 1930–1960* (New Haven, CT: Yale University Press, 1989). The historian Cynthia Orozco has argued that Mexican American Generation activists and their struggle for civil rights originated not in the 1930s but a decade earlier. See Orozco, *No Mexicans, Women, or Dogs Allowed: The Rise of the Mexican American Civil Rights Movement* (Austin: University of Texas Press, 2010).

5. Benjamin Márquez, *Constructing Identities in Mexican American Political Organizations: Choosing Issues, Taking Sides* (Austin: University of Texas Press, 2003), 1–4; F. Arturo Rosales, *Chicano! The History of the Mexican American Civil Rights Movement*, 2nd ed. (Houston: Arte Público Press, 1997), 89–110.

6. Anthony Quiroz, *Claiming Citizenship: Mexican Americans in Victoria, Texas* (College Station: Texas A&M University Press, 2005), xvii; Quiroz, *Leaders of the Mexican American Generation: Biographical Essays* (Boulder: University Press of Colorado, 2015), 5.

7. Congress and the courts constructed Mexican-origin people as white for citizenship purposes. Mexican American activists used this classification to pursue equality and full citizenship rights from 1929 to 1960. For the legal construction of Mexicans as white see Ian F. Haney-López, *White by Law: The Legal Construction of Race* (New York: New York University Press, 1996); and George A. Martínez, "The Legal Construction of Race: Mexican Americans and Whiteness," *Harvard Latino Law Review* 2 (1997): 321–47. Guadalupe San Miguel Jr. has shown how Mexican Americans used the whiteness strategy to challenge school segregation in Texas. See *Let All of Them Take Heed: Mexican Americans and the Quest for Educational Equality in Texas, 1910–1981* (College Station: Texas A&M University Press, 2002). For a brief discussion of the debate over whiteness in the Mexican American civil rights movement see Carlos K. Blanton, "George I. Sánchez, Ideology, and Whiteness in the Making of the Mexican American Civil Rights Movement, 1930–1960," *Journal of Southern History* 72, no. 3 (August 2006): 572–76.

8. On the Mexican American Generation and the new identity it embraced see García, *Mexican Americans*; Quiroz, *Claiming Citizenship*, xv–xxv, and *Leaders of the Mexican American Generation*, 1–21; and Rosales, *Chicano!* 89–110.

9. A minority of activists, especially those involved in working-class organizations such as the Asociación Nacional México-Americana (ANMA), on occasion engaged in direct action tactics such as boycotts, marches, and rallies. See García, *Mexican Americans*.

10. For two studies illustrating the importance of the Mexican American Generation and its use of conventional methods to bring about moderate social

reform in Victoria, Texas, and in public education in Texas, see Quiroz, *Claiming Citizenship*; and San Miguel, *Let All of Them Take Heed*, respectively.

11. For the role that the Community Service Organization (CSO) played in contesting discrimination in northern California and in Arizona during the post-WWII years see Stephen J. Pitti, *The Devil in Silicon Valley: Northern California, Race and Mexican Americans* (Princeton: Princeton University Press, 2003), 148–172. On Mexican American struggles against discrimination in southern California in this era see José M. Alamillo, *Making Lemonade Out of Lemons: Mexican American Labor and Leisure in a California Town, 1880–1960* (Chicago: University of Illinois Press, 2006), 142–67; and George J. Sánchez, *Becoming Mexican American: Ethnicity, Culture, and Identity in Chicano Los Angeles, 1900–1945* (New York: Oxford University Press, 1995).

12. García, *Mexican Americans*; Quiroz, *Claiming Citizenship*; San Miguel, *Let All of Them Take Heed*; Rosales, *Chicano*; Orozco, *No Mexicans, Women, or Dogs Allowed*.

13. Mario García argues that Mexican Americans could do little to overcome these barriers. Without addressing their own internal limitations, rigorously advancing the class struggle, and thwarting the oppressive cold war politics of the 1950s, they could not dismantle racism and structural discrimination. See García, *Mexican Americans*, 298.

## CHAPTER 1

1. San Miguel, *Let All of Them Take Heed*; García, *Mexican Americans*.

2. Ignacio M. García, *Viva Kennedy!* (College Station: Texas A&M University Press, 2000), 92.

3. For further information on Telles, see Mario T. García, *The Making of a Mexican American Mayor: Raymond L. Telles of El Paso* (Tucson: University of Arizona Press, 2018).

4. Earlier both Henry B. González and Hector P. García had been offered ambassadorships, but their existing professional and political responsibilities precluded them from accepting them. Julie Leininger Pycior, *LBJ & Mexican Americans: The Paradox of Power* (Austin: University of Texas Press, 1997), 122; García, *Viva Kennedy!* 111–40.

5. Pycior, *LBJ & Mexican Americans*, 123.

6. See Louise Ann Fisch, *All Rise: Reynaldo G. Garza, The First Mexican American Federal Judge* (College Station: Texas A&M University Press, 1996).

7. Kennedy appointed Garza on March 23, and the Senate confirmed him on April 13. Pycior, *LBJ & Mexican Americans*, 124.

8. Pycior, *LBJ & Mexican Americans*, 123–24.

9. Carlos McCormick, Peña, and García called this meeting. Teresa Palomo Acosta, "Political Association of Spanish-Speaking Organizations," Handbook

of Texas Online, https://www.tshaonline.org/handbook/entries/political-asso
ciation-of-spanish-speaking-organizations.

10. Activists in California also denounced the Democratic Party's failure to
consistently support Mexican American candidates for political office and
political issues important to their community. In the 1950s, for instance,
the California Democratic Party failed to support two prominent Mexican
Americans running for statewide office. In 1954 the party refused to support Edward Roybal for lieutenant governor, supposedly because there was
already a Catholic on the ticket. Four years later, Democratic Party leaders
failed to support Hank López for secretary of state because they believed his
Mexican background would make him an unpopular candidate. Seeking to
combat discrimination in the Democratic Party, activists formed the Mexican
American Political Association. See Mario T. García, *Memories of Chicano
History: The Life and Narrative of Bert Corona* (Berkeley: University of California Press, 1994), 195–206.

11. Carlos McCormick originally called this meeting to continue the momentum of
the Viva Kennedy clubs after the 1960 election. García, *Viva Kennedy!* 123.

12. García, *Viva Kennedy!* 125–26.

13. García, *Viva Kennedy!* 126–28.

14. For a fascinating view of the organization's diverse views and the debates over
endorsing a candidate for governor, see I. García, *Viva Kennedy!* 123–59.

15. Shockley, *Chicano Revolt in a Texas Town.*

16. Ignacio M. García, *Hector P. García: In Relentless Pursuit of Justice* (Houston,
TX: Arte Público Press, 2002), 24.

17. Pycior, *LBJ & Mexican Americans*, 128–29.

18. Pycior, *LBJ & Mexican Americans*, 129.

19. Pycior, *LBJ & Mexican Americans*, 131.

20. George A. Martínez reviewed several court cases in the early twentieth
century that ruled racially mixed people in general were not white. With
respect to Mexican Americans, however, in a naturalization case in 1897, in
integration cases between 1930 and 1954, and in jury discrimination cases in
the 1940s and 1950s, the courts ruled that Mexican Americans were legally
white. On the federal level, the Census Bureau and the Office of Management and Budget also constructed Mexican Americans as white during the
early and mid-1900s. For further information see Martínez, "Legal Construction of Race"; see also Haney-López, *White by Law.*

21. See, for example, the various presentations made at the October Cabinet
Committee Hearings on Mexican American Affairs found in *The Mexican
American, A New Focus on Opportunity* (Washington, DC: Inter-Agency
Committee on Mexican American Affairs, 1968).

22. García, *Hector P. García*, 256–58.

23. Pycior, *LBJ & Mexican Americans*, 146.

24. See Rodríguez, *Rethinking the Chicano Movement*, chap 2.

25. The president initially met with Mexican American leaders in March 1965 to discuss their concerns, but nothing significant came of this meeting. Pycior, *LBJ & Mexican Americans*, 154. On the April meeting, see AGIF, "Testimony on the Office of Economic Opportunity Submitted by Rudy Ramos, Director of the Washington, D.C., Office of the American G.I. Forum," April 26, 1965. See also AGIF, *Anatomy of a Presidential Statement on Equal Employment Opportunity and Civil Rights for Mexican Americans, 1966* (report, Washington, DC: AGIF, 1966). Both documents were provided to the author by Hector P. García and are now located in the Hector P. García Archives, Texas A&M University, Corpus Christi. For a brief narrative of this events, see Carl Allsup, *The American GI Forum: Origins and Evolution* (Austin: University of Texas Press, 1982), 134–37.

26. In 1963, Mexican Americans complained to the federal government about the lack of Mexican American staff members in Neighborhood Youth Corps, one of the most important programs of the War on Poverty. LBJ tended to ignore these concerns. Others found a variety of problems with the implementation of the Neighborhood Youth Corps and other War on Poverty programs. Although helpful, they increased tensions between community groups and local or state political leaders. Governor Connally opposed these programs because he was not in control of them. LBJ was performing a balancing act between supporting his political allies like Connally and his political friends among Mexican Americans. He began to lean more towards Connally. Pycior, *LBJ & Mexican Americans*, 171–74.

27. Pycior, *LBJ & Mexican Americans*, 163.

28. Quoted in Craig A. Kaplowitz, *LULAC, Mexican Americans, and National Policy* (College Station: Texas A&M University Press, 2005), 100.

29. On March 27, 1966, one day before the EEOC conference, the southern California delegation of MAPA accused the EEOC of discrimination for failing to have a Mexican American on the five-member commission. Kaplowitz, *LULAC, Mexican Americans, and National Policy*, 100; for an overview of the walkout, see pp. 98–100. Fifty-two individuals from several organizations, including LULAC, PASSO, AGIF, MAPA, CSO, and the Latin American Civic Association (LACA), walked out. The EEOC was formed in 1964, but no commissioners were appointed until the following year after pressure from African American civil rights groups.

30. Kaplowitz, *LULAC, Mexican Americans, and National Policy*, 101, 103. Alfred Hernández (LULAC), Miguel Montes (LACA), Albert Peña (PASSO), and Augustín Flores (AGIF) each made a statement. See also Pycior, *LBJ & Mexican Americans*, 164–70.

31. Pycior, *LBJ & Mexican Americans*, 166–67; García, *Viva Kennedy*; Kaplowitz, *LULAC, Mexican Americans, and National Policy*, 101.

32. Pycior, *LBJ & Mexican Americans*, 169.
33. Kaplowitz, *LULAC, Mexican Americans, and National Policy*, 104.
34. Pycior, *LBJ & Mexican Americans*, 182.
35. Pycior, *LBJ & Mexican Americans*, 170.
36. Pycior, *LBJ & Mexican Americans*, 182.
37. For the political issues behind the selection of a new commissioner, see Kaplowitz, *LULAC, Mexican Americans, and National Policy*, 106–7, 114. In the summer of 1967, LBJ took further steps to ensure that Mexican American concerns would be integrated into the administration's agenda. He encouraged his cabinet members to hire more Mexican Americans and to direct more poverty programs to Spanish-speaking communities throughout the nation. A few AGIF members were appointed to the Advisory Committee on Community Relations Service, a civil rights committee established under Title X of the Civil Rights Act of 1964. In 1966 President Johnson appointed a few Mexican Americans to higher profile positions in the OEO. He promised to make further appointments after Hector García called for a Mexican American presidential assistant to establish better communications between advocacy organizations and the federal government. Allsup, *American G.I. Forum*, 137.
38. *The Mexican American: A New Focus on Opportunity*, viii.
39. See Lyndon Baines Johnson, Memo to Secretaries of Labor, HEW, Agriculture, Housing and Urban Development, Director of Office of Economic Opportunity, and Vicente Ximenes, June 9, 1967, FG 687 Inter-Agency Committee on Mexican-American Affairs, Box 39, LBJ Library. Congress later sanctioned this action by passing legislation creating a federal agency whose purpose was to ensure that federal programs were reaching Mexican Americans. This federal agency underwent several name changes. See José E. Vega, *Education, Politics, and Bilingualism in Texas* (Washington, DC: University Press of America, 1983), 29; Armando Rendón, "La Raza—Today Not Manana," *Civil Rights Digest* (Spring 1968): 7–10; reprinted in *Mexican-Americans in the United States: A Reader*, ed. John H. Burma (Cambridge, MA: Schenkman, 1970), 309. In 1969, the name was changed to the Cabinet Committee on Opportunities for the Spanish Speaking People to be inclusive of other Latinas/os. See P.L. 91–81, 83 Stat. 838 (1969) and 42 U.S.C., Sec. 4301 (Supp. V, 1970).
40. Speeches given by Vicente Ximenes, 1969–1971 Folder, Papers of Vicente T. Ximenes, Box 1, LBJ Library.
41. The HEW secretary wrote to the president on February 11, 1967, that he did not favor holding a White House conference on Mexican American civil rights. "The truth is that White House Conferences are inevitably risky with groups of this sort," he noted. "The temptation is great to use the conference as a means of belaboring the Administration." Instead, he recommended

creating some type of committee on Mexican Americans that would seek to meet their needs over time. See Secretary of HEW, Memorandum for the President, February 11, 1967, Mexican American Conference Folder, Box 7, Irvine Sprague Papers, LBJ Library.

42. In his recollections, Ximenes stated that he, not his aides or LBJ, decided to hold the hearings in El Paso. See Vicente Ximenes, Speech to the Philosophers Club of Albuquerque, November 7, 2003, p. 2, Speeches given by Vicente Ximenes, 1969–1971 Folder, Box 1, LBJ Library.

43. Allsup, *American G.I. Forum.*

44. Press Conference of Vicente Ximenes, Chair, Inter-Agency Committee on Mexican-American Affairs, September 12, 1967, Mexican American Conference Folder, Irvine Sprague Papers. Although the hearing was officially announced in September, Ximenes told the AGIF members at their national conference on August 4 that he was considering holding public hearings on Mexican American problems shortly. See Peter Esquivel, Press Release, American G.I. Forum, August 4, 1967, Denver, CO, Mexican American Conference Folder, Irvine Sprague Papers.

45. At least two major meetings were held to discuss this issue. One was in Malibu, California, in early October; the other one in Albuquerque, New Mexico, a week before the hearings. For a review of these two meetings and the decisions made there, see "Protesting the El Paso Conference," *La Raza*, October 15, 1967, reprinted in *Testimonio: A Documentary History of the Mexican American Struggle for Civil Rights*, ed. F. Arturo Rosales (Houston, TX: Arte Público Press, 2000), 325–26, and "Young Organizers Meet in New Mexico," *La Raza*, October 29, 1967, reprinted in Rosales, *Testimonio*, 305. The leaders of what would become MAYO also met to discuss what they should do. See García, *United We Win*, 20.

46. Rosales, *Chicano!* 166–67; for MAPA's decision to boycott, see Phil R. Ortiz to Vicente T. Ximenes, October 19, 1967, FG 687 Inter-Agency Committee on Mexican-American Affairs Folder, Ximenes Papers.

47. See "Young Organizers Meet in New Mexico," in Rosales, *Testimonio*; and García, *United We Win*, 20.

48. García, *Memories of Chicano History*, 225.

49. Undersecretary of Labor James J. Reynolds attended on behalf of Wirtz, who could not attend. See *Mexican American: A New Focus on Opportunity*, 39.

50. For a list of topics and speakers, see Participants, Cabinet Committee Hearings on Mexican American Affairs, Program, El Paso, TX, October 26–28, 1967, FG 687 Inter-Agency Committee on Mexican-American Affairs, Ximenes Papers.

51. Eight individuals presented before the secretary of agriculture, nine before the secretary of labor, eleven before the secretary of HEW, eight before the secretary of HUD, nine before the director of the EEOC, and six before

Commissioner Ximenes. See list of presenters in *Mexican American: A New Focus on Opportunity*, xiii–xiv.

52. For examples of presenters with extremely critical views of the federal government, see the following speeches in *Mexican American: A New Focus on Opportunity*: Ernesto Galarza, "Rural Community Development," 1–3; Dr. Clark S. Knowlton, "Among the Spanish Americans," 233–38; Ralph Guzmán, "Mexican American," 245–49, and Commissioner Albert A. Peña, "The Mexican American and the War on Poverty," 211–13.

53. The opening statement of Daniel R. López, manager, East Los Angeles Service Center, reporting on legislative recommendations for the War on Poverty, is illustrative of the respectful way in which most Mexican American leaders viewed their opportunity to be heard. "This paper has been prepared at the request of the office of the Honorable Vicente T. Ximenes, Chairman of the Inter-Agency Committee on Mexican-American Affairs," he began. "I am grateful and honored by this most generous invitation." See López, "Legislative Recommendations for the War on Poverty," in *Mexican American: A New Focus on Opportunity*, 189.

54. *Mexican American: A New Focus on Opportunity*, xi.

55. Quoted in Rendón, "La Raza—Today Not Manana," 316.

56. *Mexican American: A New Focus on Opportunity*, xi.

57. Press release, Report to President Johnson, January 25, 1968, FG 687, Inter-Agency Committee on Mexican-American Affairs Folder, Box 39, Vicente T. Ximenes Papers.

58. Press release, Report to President Johnson, Ximenes Papers.

59. For one of several hearings on bilingual education in the 1967 session, see U.S. Congress, Senate, Committee on Labor and Public Welfare, Special Sub-committee on Bilingual Education, Hearings on S. 428, 90th Congress (Washington, DC: Government Printing Office, 1967).

60. See, for instance, the following speeches in *Mexican American: A New Focus on Opportunity*: Hercelia Toscano, "Bilingual Education," 115–16; Nick E. Garza, "Bilingualism in Education," 117–18; Julian Nava, "Educational Problems of Mexican Americans," 97–99; and Edward V. Moreno, "Elementary and Secondary Education," 105.

61. Rodríguez stated mistakenly that there were only three—the Inter-Agency Committee on Mexican-American Affairs, the U.S.-Mexico Commission on Border Development and Friendship, and the Mexican American Affairs Unit in the U.S. Office of Education—but there were at least four. See Armando M. Rodríguez, "Speak Up Chicano," *American Education* (May 1968): 7–9. Reprinted as "Speak Up Chicano: The Mexican American Fights for Educational Equality," in Burma, *Mexican-Americans in the United States*, 135–40.

62. In the early 1970s, President Richard M. Nixon appointed Ramírez to chair the former Inter-Agency Committee on Mexican American Affairs, now

renamed the Committee on the Opportunities for the Spanish Speaking. For Ramírez's own words on his appointment to this position, see *Chicano in the White House.*

63. Data were compiled in three phases: A stratified random sample of all school districts in the United States; a mail survey of 538 districts and 1,166 schools throughout the Southwest; and a field study of 52 schools in California, New Mexico, and Texas.

64. This interpretation, based on the 1966 Coleman Report, argued that school conditions and practices had little effect on achievement. Instead, the most important factors in student success were family support and student peers. (This premise was later questioned, but it was the basis for desegregation.) See James S. Coleman, *Equality of Educational Opportunity* (Washington, DC: Government Printing Office, 1966).

65. For a summary of these reports and their importance to the education of Mexican Americans, see Susan Navarro Uranga, "The Study of Mexican American Education in the Southwest: Implications of Research by the Civil Rights Commission," Washington, DC, U.S. Commission on Civil Rights, 1972, ERIC document 070 545 RC 006 617.

66. In one of the many articles he wrote, Rodríguez noted that many parents and youth were showing pride in their heritage, speaking up against discrimination in the schools, and calling for changes in how school officials dealt with Mexican American children and parents. Despite this growing awareness and involvement, however, he argued that three major obstacles to a successful comprehensive education for Mexican American children remained: a shortage of bilingual teachers, the lack of well-integrated curricula, and a lack of role models or heroes. He was accompanied on this listening tour by Lupe Anguiano and Dean Bistline. See Rodríguez, "Speak Up Chicano."

67. Marlena Fitzpatrick, "Lupe Anguiano: A Life Devoted to Social Justice," Latino Rebels, March 9, 2016, http://www.latinorebels.com/2016/03/09/lupe-anguiano-a-life-devoted-to-social-justice.

68. According to the historian Julie Leininger Pycior, Johnson was antagonistic toward women and refused to include them in meetings. This attitude plus her lack of academic credentials might be the reasons why Anguiano was not selected to head this unit. See Pycior, *LBJ & Mexican Americans*, 152–53.

69. "Anguiano, Lupe," Social Networks and Archival Content, http://socialarchive.iath.virginia.edu/ark:/99166/w66h55v1.

70. Miguel Montes, a dentist from San Fernando, CA, chaired the committee and Armando Rodríguez served as administrative director. The other members were Edward E. Booher, president of McGraw-Hill in New York, Clayton Brace, vice president and general manager of Time-Life Broadcast in San Diego, CA; Reverend Henry J. Casso, vicar of urban affairs at St. John's Seminary in San Antonio, TX; Jack P. Crowther, a school superintendent

from Los Angeles, CA; Ernestine D. Evans, New Mexico secretary of state, Santa Fe; Nick Garza, principal of Sidney Lanier High School, San Antonio, TX; Ralph Guzmán, LA State College, Los Angeles, CA; Alfred J. Hernández, judge in the Corporation Court, Houston, TX; Frank Hubert, dean of the College of Arts and Sciences, Texas A&M University, College Station; Leonard C. Lane of New York; Eloy Martínez of HELP, Española, NM; farmer Jesse G. Stratton, chairman of the executive board, Southwest Cooperative Educational Laboratory, Clinton, OK; María Urquides, dean of girls at Pueblo High School, Tucson, AZ. See National Advisory Committee on Mexican American Education, *The Mexican American: Quest for Equality* (Albuquerque, NM, Southwestern Educational Laboratory, 1968).

71. National Advisory Committee on Mexican American Education, *Mexican American: Quest for Equality.*

72. García, *Hector P. García.*

73. U.S. Commission on Civil Rights, *Hearings before the U.S. Commission on Civil Rights, Dec. 9–14, 1968, San Antonio* (Washington, DC: Government Printing Office, 1969).

74. "Report Indicates Civil Rights Panel Has Already Drawn Its Conclusions," *San Antonio Express*, December 5, 1968, 5G.

75. U.S. Commission on Civil Rights, *Hearings*; See also "Report Indicates Civil Rights Panel Has Already Drawn Its Conclusions."

76. Office of the White House Press Secretary, the White House, President Reports on Actions to Aid Spanish-Speaking Citizens (draft), January 1968, Box 1, Ximenes Papers, LBJ Library.

77. Office of the White House Press Secretary, Statement by the President, February 23, 1968. Mexican American Conference Folder, Box 7, Irvine Sprague Papers, LBJ library.

78. By January 1968, HUD had designated a number of model cities, "including 29 locations in the Southwest, many of them with large Mexican American populations, Spanish Harlem, and Puerto Rico." See Press Release, Report to President Johnson, January 25, 1968, p. 2, Box 1, Ximenes Papers, LBJ Library.

79. "National Hispanic Heritage Month," Library of Congress, updated December 30, 2020, http://www.loc.gov/law/help/commemorative-observations/hispanic-heritage.php.

80. National Hispanic Heritage Week, P.L. 90-498, September 17, 1968; see also "The Creation and Evolution of the National Hispanic Heritage Celebration," U.S. House of Representatives, September 17, 1968, http://history.house.gov/HistoricalHighlight/Detail/15032398402; and "National Hispanic Heritage Month," Library of Congress. For a draft of the bill submitted to Congress see Draft of bill to Establish the Committee on Mexican American Affairs, sent to Hubert H. Humphrey, President of the Senate and John W. McCormack,

Speaker of the Hose of Representatives, by Vicente T. Ximenes, January 1, 1968, FG 687, Inter-Agency Committee on Mexican-American Affairs, Ximenes Papers, LBJ Library.

81. Ximenes to Mr. Robertson, February 19, 1968, Box 1, Ximenes Papers, LBJ Library; A. Ross Eckler, Director, Census Bureau, to Vicente T. Ximenes, May 23, 1969, Box 1, Ximenes Papers.

## CHAPTER 2

1. The radical tradition of activism has been a minor but important one in Mexican American history, alongside the dominant tradition of moderation. Mexican American activists have accepted mainstream institutions and used legal means to challenge, oppose, or protest social injustice and unequal treatment. They have lobbied political leaders, petitioned the courts, written editorials, mobilized "juntas de indignación" (indignation meetings), and made moral and religious arguments against defamation, segregation, social injustice, and institutional mistreatment. For one dated study of the moderate and radical traditions of activism in Chicana/o history, see Armando Navarro, "The Evolution of Chicano Politics," *Aztlan* 5, nos. 1–2 (1974): 57–84. For a different view see David Montejano, *Anglos and Mexicans in the Making of Texas, 1836–1986* (Austin: University of Texas Press, 1987).

2. Robert J. Rosenbaum, *Mexicano Resistance in the Southwest* (Dallas, TX: Southern Methodist University Press, 2018).

3. See, for instance, the proclamation issued by Las Gorras Blancas in 1890: "Las Gorras Blancas," in Rosales, *Testimonio*, 29–30.

4. On Gregorio Cortez, see Américo Paredes, *With His Pistol in His Hand: A Border Ballad and Its Hero* (Austin: University of Texas Press, 1958). On the Plan de San Diego, see Benjamin Heber Johnson, *Revolution in Texas: How a Forgotten Rebellion and Its Bloody Suppression Turned Mexicans into Americans* (New Haven, CT: Yale University Press, 2005), 5.

5. Rosales, *Chicano*, chaps. 2–5; F. Arturo Rosales, *¡Pobre Raza! Violence, Justice, and Mobilization among México Lindo Immigrants, 1900–1936* (Austin: University of Texas Press, 1999); Juan Gómez-Quiñones, *Sembradores: Ricardo Flores Magón y el Partido Liberal Mexicano* (Los Angeles, CA: UCLA Chicano Studies Research Center Publications, 1973); Justin Akers Chacón, *Radicals in the Barrio: Magonistas, Socialists, Wobblies, and Communists in the Mexican American Working Class* (Chicago: Haymarket Books, 2018), chaps. 7–14; Johnson, *Revolution in Texas*; Juan Gómez-Quiñones, "The First Steps: Chicano Labor Conflict and Organizing, 1900–1920," *Aztlan* 3 (Spring 1972); Emilio Zamora, *The World of the Mexican Worker in Texas* (College Station: Texas A&M University Press, 1993); José Amaro Hernández, *Mutual Aid for Survival: The Case of the Mexican American* (Malabar, FL: Robert E. Krieger, 1983), chap. 2.

6. García, *Mexican Americans*, chaps. 6–8. For a comprehensive view of radical working-class organizations and labor unions in the Southwest from the late 1800s to the 1950s see Chacón, *Radicals in the Barrio*.

7. García, *Mexican Americans*, 159–65, 173–74. For another view of El Congreso see Chacón, *Radicals in the Barrio*, 541–54.

8. García, *Mexican Americans*, 165.

9. This committee defended the rights of Mexican American youths wrongly accused of killing another individual at a local party in East Los Angeles near a reservoir known as the Sleepy Lagoon. For information on the causes and consequences of this event, see Eduardo Obregón Pagán, *Murder at the Sleepy Lagoon: Zoot Suits, Race, and Riot in Wartime L.A.* (Durham: University of North Carolina Press, 2003).

10. García, *Mexican Americans*, 173.

11. Rudy Acuña described how the CIO was more receptive than the AFL to organizing farmworkers, Mexican Americans, and African Americans. See Rodolfo Acuña, *Occupied America: A History of Chicanos*, 5th ed. (New York: Pearson, 2004), 219.

12. García, *Mexican Americans*, 176–80.

13. García, *Mexican Americans*, 186–90.

14. García, *Mexican Americans*, 191–96, 199–230.

15. García, *Mexican Americans*, 218–19.

16. The government also opposed ANMA because it encouraged an internationalist consciousness aimed at maintaining a "Mexican" and "Latin American" connection and a domestic front that united progressive whites, labor unions, middle-class Mexican Americans, leftist organizations, and African Americans. Mario García argues that the group was probably part of the Communist Party's popular front strategy. It was viewed as the political arm of the Mexican American communities of the Southwest. See García, *Mexican Americans*, 200, 222–26.

17. García, *Mexican Americans*, 207. For a different view of ANMA, see Chacón, *Radicals in the Barrio*, 541–54.

18. He also persuaded Gil Padilla to resign from the CSO and join him in forming the NFWA. Rosales, *Chicano*, 132. Matt García, *From the Jaws of Victory: The Triumph and Tragedy of César Chávez and the Farm Worker Movement* (Los Angeles: University of California Press, 2012), 31.

19. About two-fifths of workers walked out. Rosales, *Chicano*, 136.

20. Matt S. Meier and Feliciano Ribera, *The Chicanos: A History of Mexican Americans* (New York: Hill and Wang, 1972), 262.

21. Mahatma Gandhi first made this statement, but Chávez, who was greatly influenced by Gandhi's philosophy of nonviolence, reiterated it. Many of Chávez's statements are now quoted on popular websites. For example, see

"César Chávez Quotes, March 31, 1927–April 23, 1993," BrainyQuote, https://www.brainyquote.com/authors/César_Chávez.

22. A number of books on the history of the farmworker movement and on César Chávez have been published. A few examples are Richard Griswold del Castillo and Richard García, *César Chávez: A Triumph of Spirit* (Norman: University of Oklahoma Press, 1995); Susan Ferris and Ricardo Sandoval, *The Fight in the Fields: César Chávez and the Farmworkers Movement* (New York: Harcourt Brace, 1997); Mario T. García, ed., *The Gospel of César Chávez: My Faith in Action* (Lanham, MD: Sheed & Ward, 2007); Miriam Pawel, *The Union of Their Dreams: Power, Hope, and Struggle in César Chávez's Farm Worker Movement* (New York: Bloomsbury Press, 2009); Randy Shaw, *Beyond the Fields: César Chávez, the UFW, and the Struggle for Justice in the 21st Century* (Berkeley: University of California Press, 2008); García, *From the Jaws of Victory*.

23. This action encouraged organizers in other states to conduct their own marches. In Texas, protesters marched four hundred miles from South Texas to the capital in Austin to publicize their campaign for a minimum wage and improved working conditions for farmworkers. See Marilyn D. Rhinehart and Thomas H. Kreneck, "The Minimum Wage March of 1966: A Case Study in Mexican-American Politics, Labor, and Identity," *Houston Review* 11, no. 1 (1989): 27–33.

24. A copy of this plan is in Luis Valdez and Stan Steiner, eds., *Aztlan: An Anthology of Mexican American Literature* (New York: Vintage Books, 1972), 197–201. See also "Commentary of Luis Valdez: The Plan of Delano," UC San Diego Library, https://libraries.ucsd.edu/farmworkermovement/essays/essays/Plan%20of%20Delano.pdf.

25. Ferris and Sandoval, *Fight in the Fields*, 96, 97.

26. Ferris and Sandoval, *Fight in the Fields*, 142–46.

27. Ferris and Sandoval, *Fight in the Fields*, 97.

28. On the evolution of this boycott, see Ferris and Sandoval, *Fight in the Fields*, 125–54; and García, *From the Jaws of Victory*, 44–112.

29. Strangely enough, few studies have been done on Dolores Huerta and the role she played in the UFW struggle. For one insightful study, see Mario T. García, *A Dolores Huerta Reader* (Albuquerque: University of New México Press, 2008).

30. Chávez, with his philosophy of nonviolent civil disobedience, and Huerta with her negotiating skills and devotion to farmworkers' families, mobilized farmworkers to seek recognition of the union, increased wages (from $1.10 to $1.25 per hour, or from 10 cents to 25 cents per box of grapes), and improved conditions in the fields. Their struggle was interpreted as a fight for social and economic justice. Meier and Ribera, *Chicanos*, 262.

31. García, *Chicanismo*, 31.
32. "Luis Valdez," Wikimedia Foundation, last modified February 26, 2021, https://en.wikipedia.org/wiki/Luis_Valdez.
33. Rosales, *Chicano*, 136.
34. Paredes, *With His Pistol in His Hand*, 129–30.
35. For an overview of corridos, canciones, and other types of music in the history of Mexican Americans in Texas, see Guadalupe San Miguel Jr., *Tejano Proud: Tex-Mex Music in the Twentieth Century* (College Station: Texas A&M University Press, 2002), 3–19.
36. For more on Valdez's writings and influences see the great interview "This Is Us!—Luis Valdez," YouTube, last updated January 20, 2009, https://www.youtube.com/watch?v=isPFm9A_xRM.
37. Valdez and Steiner, *Aztlan*, 197–201.
38. Patricia Bell Blawis, *Tijerina and the Land Grants: Mexican Americans in Struggle for Their Heritage* (New York: International Publishers, 1971), 39; Rosales, *Chicano*, 158.
39. Blawis, *Tijerina and the Land Grants*, 48–55. For Tijerina's own words, see Reies López Tijerina, *They Called Me "King Tiger": My Struggle for the Land and Our Rights* (Houston, TX: Arte Público Press, 2000).
40. Blawis, *Tijerina and the Land Grants*, 31–56; Rosales, *Chicano*, 159–60.
41. Blawis, *Tijerina and the Land Grants*, 56–68; Rosales, *Chicano*, 160–61.
42. The attorney general had been jailing Alianza members for attending organizational meetings. Rosales, *Chicano*, 162.
43. Blawis, *Tijerina and the Land Grants*, 69–97; Rosales, *Chicano*, 162–65.
44. For a discussion of these efforts see Mariscal, *Brown-Eyed Children of the Sun*, 171–209, and Blawis, *Tijerina and the Land Grants*, 131–44.
45. "Young Organizers Meet in New Mexico," *La Raza*, October 29, 1967, reprinted in Rosales, *Testimonio*, 305.
46. Rodolfo Gonzales, *I Am Joaquín/Yo Soy Joaquín* (New York: Bantam Books, 1972).
47. Blawis, *Tijerina and the Land Grants*, 116–30; Tijerina, *They Called Me "King Tiger."*
48. Antonio Esquibel, ed. *Message to Aztlán: Selected Writings of Rodolfo "Corky" Gonzales* (Houston, TX: Arte Público Press, 2001), 32–34. A shorter version can be found in Rodolfo "Corky" Gonzales, "We Demand: Statement of Chicanos in the Southwest on the Poor People's Campaign," in Valdez and Steiner, *Aztlan*, 218–21.
49. As a young woman Flores contracted tuberculosis and spent almost a decade in a sanitarium in San Diego, California. During her stay there, she helped found an organization called the Hermanas de la Revolución. The purpose of this sisterhood was to provide a safe space for women nurses to talk about politics, discuss their working conditions, and advocate for increased wages.

See Hadley Meares, "Activist and Journalist Francisca Flores Is a Chicana Hero Every Angeleno Should Know," *Los Angeles Magazine*, November 26, 2018, https://www.lamag.com/citythinkblog/francisca-flores/.

50. Meares, "Activist and Journalist Francisca Flores," is an excellent article on Flores's early years.

51. Whereas male-dominated Mexican American organizations did not promote women as leaders, the Democratic Party in the 1950s did. Ramona Tijerina Morin, for instance, became the chairwoman of the Democratic Women Committee of the East Los Angeles–Belvedere club. Elected officials also appointed her to the Democratic Party State Central Committee. Anna NietoGomez, "Francisca Flores, the League of Mexican American Women, and the Comisión Femenil Mexicana Nacional, 1958–1975," in *Chicana Movidas: New Narratives of Activism and Feminism in the Movement Era*, ed. Dionne Espinoza, María Eugenia Cotera, and Maylei Blackwell (Austin: University of Texas Press, 2018), 37.

52. Morin's husband wrote a book about the experiences of Mexican Americans in World War II and the Korean War. See Raul Morin, *Among the Valiant: Mexican-Americans in WW II and Korea* (Los Angeles, CA: Borden, 1963).

53. NietoGomez, "Francisca Flores," 37, 39.

54. For an overview of some of the award recipients, see NietoGomez, "Francisca Flores," 40–42. On the pressure to appoint women, see 38–43.

55. For one major instance of sexism by Mexican American male leaders in 1963, see Francisca Flores and Delfino Varela, "Women and Dogs Not Allowed," *Carta Editorial* 1, no. 9 (August 6, 1963), 2.

56. Flores founded two additional national feminist organizations during the 1970s that supported Chicano Movement leaders and activities and continued empowering Chicanas to address their specific concerns: Comisión Femenil Mexicana Nacional and the Chicana Service Action Center. On her role in their establishment, see NietoGomez, "Francisca Flores," 44–50.

57. On MAYO see Navarro, *Mexican American Youth Organization*. On the emerging Chicano student movement see Juan Gómez-Quiñones, *Mexican Students por La Raza: The Chicano Student Movement in Southern California, 1967–1977* (Santa Barbara, CA: Editorial La Causa, 1978).

58. Navarro, *Mexican American Youth Organization*.

59. Rendón, "La Raza—Today Not Manana," 307–26.

60. For an overview of the literature on the L.A. walkouts, see F. Arturo Rosales, "The Fight for Educational Reform," in *Chicano*, 175–95; Dolores Delgado Bernal, "Chicana School Resistance and Grassroots Leadership: Providing an Alternative History of the 1968 East Los Angeles Blowouts" (PhD diss., University of California, Los Angeles, 1997); Kaye Briegel, "Chicano Student Militancy: The Los Angeles High School Strike of 1968," in *An Awakened*

*Minority: The Mexican Americans*, ed. Manuel P. Servin (New York: Macmillan, 1974); Carlos Muñoz Jr., "The Politics of Protest and Chicano Liberation: A Case Study of Repression and Cooperation," *Aztlan* 5, nos. 1–2 (1974); Muñoz, "The Politics of Educational Change in East Los Angeles," in *Mexican Americans and Educational Change*, ed. Alfredo Castañeda et al. (New York: Arno Press, 1974).

61. Mario T. García and Sal Castro, *Blowout: Sal Castro and the Chicano Struggle for Educational Justice* (Chapel Hill: University of North Carolina Press, 2011).

62. Muñoz, "Politics of Educational Change," 86.

63. On the walkouts in Denver see, e.g., Vigil, *Crusade for Justice*, 81–87. On the Chicago protests, see Carmen María Torres Sánchez, "An Historical Inquiry into the Role of Community Activist Organizations in Dealing with the Problem of Overcrowded Elementary Schools in the Hispanic Community of Chicago, 1970–1990" (EdD diss., Northern Illinois University, 1993).

64. Elaine Ayala, "San Antonio, 1968," *Chicago Tribune*, May 7, 2008, https://www.chicagotribune.com/news/ct-xpm-2008-05-07-0805050204-story.html.

65. On student protests in Texas, see Navarro, *Mexican American Youth Organization*, 115–48; and Baldemar James Barrera, "'We Want Better Education!': The Chicano Student Movement for Educational Reform in South Texas, 1968–1970" (PhD diss., University of New Mexico, May 2007. For information on walkouts in particular cities, see Juan O. Sánchez, "Walkout Cabrones: The Uvalde School Walkout of 1970," *West Texas Historical Association Year Book* 68(1992); Sánchez, "Encina: The Uvalde School Walkout" (master's thesis, Sul Ross State University, 1992); Guadalupe San Miguel Jr., "The Community Is Beginning to Rumble: The Origins of Chicano Educational Protest in Houston, 1965–1970," *Houston Review* 13, no. 3 (1991); Miguel A. Guajardo and Francisco J. Guajardo, "The Impact of Brown on the Brown of South Texas: A Micropolitical Perspective on the Education of Mexican Americans in a South Texas Community," *American Educational Research Journal* 41, no. 3 (2004); Baldemar James Barrera, "Edcouch-Elsa High School Walkout: Chicano Student Activism in a South Texas Community" (master's thesis, University of Texas, El Paso, 2001); and Barrera, "The 1968 San Antonio School Walkouts: The Beginning of the Chicano Student Movement in South Texas," *Journal of South Texas* 21, no. 1 (2008).

66. Rosales, "Fight for Educational Reform," 175–95.

67. For information on the walkout in Kingsville, see Navarro, *Mexican American Youth Organization*, 115–48.

68. Muñoz, "Politics of Educational Change," and "Politics of Protest and Chicano Liberation."

69. On Rancho Cucamonga, see Armando Navarro, "Educational Change through Political Action." On Crystal City, see Navarro, *Mexican American Youth*

*Organization*, 115–48, and *Cristal Experiment*. On Houston see Guadalupe San Miguel Jr., *Brown, Not White: School Integration and the Chicano Movement* (College Station: Texas A&M University Press, 2001). On Uvalde see Sánchez, "Walkout Cabrones" and "Encina." On Edcouch-Elsa see Barrera, "Edcouch-Elsa High School Walkout."

## CHAPTER 3

1. "Rodolfo 'Corky' Gonzales Speaks Out," in Rosales, *Testimonio*.
2. García, *Chicanismo*; San Miguel, *Brown, Not White*.
3. García, *Chicano Movement*; Rodríguez, *Rethinking the Chicano Movement*. See also, more generally, Terry H. Anderson, *The Movement and the Sixties: Protest in America from Greensboro to Wounded Knee* (New York: Oxford University Press, 1995).
4. For insightful responses of several activists who attended this conference, see the video titled *Chicano! Quest for a Homeland*, 33:00–37:00 minutes into video, YouTube, April 7, 2012, https://www.youtube.com/watch?v=W6KcMdYwJkQ.
5. For two examples of this literature, originally published in the 1960s and 1970s, see Albert Memmi, *The Colonizer and the Colonized* (Boston: Beacon Press, 1991); and Franz Fanon, *The Wretched of the Earth* (New York: Grove Press, 2005).
6. As several scholars have noted, the language was masculinist in nature and presented a male-oriented understanding of struggle that excluded the feminist traditions of Chicanas in the movement. See Vigil, *Crusade for Justice*, 95–104, for a critique of the language used in El Plan de Aztlán.
7. "El Plan de Aztlán," in *Aztlán*, ed. Valdez and Steiner, 402–3.
8. Gonzales's opening address at the first National Chicano Youth Liberation Conference stressed the need for Chicano liberation. See Jesús Salvador Treviño, *Eyewitness: A Filmmaker's Memoir of the Chicano Movement* (Houston, TX: Arte Público Press, 2001), 104.
9. "El Plan de Aztlán," Associated Students of the University of Arizona (ASUA), http://clubs.arizona.edu/~mecha/pages/PDFs/ElPlanDeAtzlan.pdf.
10. Treviño, *Eyewitness*, 104.
11. The plan was officially written by a group called the Chicano Coordinating Council on Higher Education.
12. Chicano Coordinating Council on Higher Education, *El Plan de Santa Barbara* (Santa Barbara: La Causa Publications, 1970), 9. For an overview of this conference, see Muñoz, *Youth, Identity, Power*, 79.
13. Strangely enough, no scholars have discussed in great detail what took place at these two conferences. The author was present at the second conference and observed or participated in many of the activities taking place during the three-day event. For a brief look at the second National Chicano Youth

Liberation Conference, see Elizabeth Sutherland Martínez and Enriqueta Longeaux y Vásquez, *Viva La Raza! The Struggle of the Mexican-American People* (New York: Doubleday, 1974), 253–56.

14. For examples of articles aimed at interpreting and clarifying some of these concepts, see Rodolfo "Corky" Gonzales, "Chicano Nationalism: The Key to Unity for La Raza," *The Militant*, March 30, 1970, reprinted in *A Documentary History of the Mexican Americans*, ed. Wayne Moquin and Charles Van Doren (New York: Bantam Books, 1971); Ysidro Ramón Macías, "The Chicano Movement," *Wilson Library Bulletin*, March 1970, also reprinted in *Documentary History of the Mexican Americans* (on Chicano cultural values and other ideas); Enriqueta Longeaux y Vásquez, "Soy Chicana Primero," in García, *Chicana Feminist Thought*, 197–99; Alicia Sandoval, "Chicana Liberation," in García, *Chicana Feminist Thought*, 204–5.

15. García, *Chicanismo*, chap. 1.

16. Scholars soon began to argue that Chicanos actively resisted the oppression or colonization they experienced. For an example of this interpretation, see Leobardo F. Estrada et al., "Chicanos in the United States: History of Exploitation and Resistance," *Daedalus* 110, no. 2 (1981).

17. Chicano Coordinating Council, *El Plan de Aztlán*, 404.

18. García, *Chicanismo*.

19. The names of the panel members have not been recorded, but Ernesto Vigil identifies Patricia Borjon as one of the women who criticized sexism at the youth conference. See Vigil, *Crusade for Justice*, 97.

20. "Resolutions from the Chicana Workshop," *La Verdad*, June 1970, 9, reprinted in García, *Chicana Feminist Thought*, 146–47.

21. Treviño, *Eyewitness*, 106.

22. "Resolutions from the Chicana Workshop."

23. This resolution angered many women. Although a few felt it was necessary to cooperate with the men, others began to publicly criticize and contest male domination of the Chicano Movement. At various subsequent local, state, and regional gatherings, they argued that cultural nationalism, as defined and practiced by men, did not lead to their liberation. Instead, it helped to maintain patriarchy in the movement and inequality between the sexes. See Lorena Oropeza and Dionne Espinoza, eds., *Enriqueta Vásquez and the Chicano Movement: Writings from El Grito del Norte* (Houston, TX: Arte Público Press, 116); Adaljiza Sosa Riddell, "Chicanas and El Movimiento," and Mirta Vidal, "New Voice of la Raza: Chicanas Speak Out," both in García, *Chicana Feminist Thought*.

24. Maylei Blackwell, *Chicana Power*.

25. Treviño noted that Marxists made their arguments at the Denver conference only to be rejected by most of those present because Marx was another

*gabacho* (pejorative term for white man). After all, it was gabachos who had stolen Chicano lands. Treviño, *Eyewitness*, 104.

26. Marxists viewed the world as consisting of two classes—the bourgeoisie (elites) and the proletariat (working classes)—in constant struggle with each other. See Estevan T. Flores, "The Mexican-Origin People in the United States and Marxist Thought in Chicano Studies," in *The Left Academy: Marxist Scholarship on American Campuses*, ed. Bertell Ollman and Edward Vernoff, 3:103–38 (New York: Praeger, 1986).

27. Mariscal, *Brown-Eyed Children of the Sun*.

28. Tatcho Mindiola, "Marxism and the Chicano Movement: Preliminary Remarks, NACCS Third Annual Conference Proceedings, 1975," San Jose State University ScholarWorks, http://scholarworks.sjsu.edu/cgi/viewcontent .cgi?article=1079&context=naccs; "The New Communist Movement: The Movement Proliferates," Encyclopedia of Anti-Revisionism On-Line, https:// www.marxists.org/history/erol/ncm-1a/index.htm; "Marxist Influences in the Chican@ Movement" (audio recording), We Are Many, June 26, 2014, https:// wearemany.org/a/2014/06/marxist-influences-in-chican-movement.

29. García, *Chicanismo*, 12, 68–85.

30. A variety of other strikes took place during the late 1960s and the 1970s. Among the ones in Texas were the Economy Furniture Company strike in Austin in 1968 and the sanitation workers' strikes in Lubbock in 1968 and 1972. There is little information on who participated in them and how Chicana and Chicano activists responded to them. See Arnoldo De León, *Mexican Americans in Texas: A Brief History*, 2nd ed. (Wheeler, IL: Harlan Davidson, 1999), 137. On the sanitation strikes see Yolanda G. Romero, "Adelante Compañeros: The Sanitation Workers' Struggle in Lubbock, Texas, 1968–1972," in *Texas Labor History*, ed. Bruce A. Glasrud and James C. Maroney, 399–404 (College Station: Texas A&M University Press, 2013).

31. By the late 1970s, the company was forced to lay off workers due to declining profits during an economic depression. De León, *Mexican Americans in Texas*, 137–38. See also Laurie Coyle, Gail Hershatter, and Emily Honig, "Women at Farrah: An Unfinished Story," in *Mexican Women in the United States: Struggles Past and Present*, ed. Magdalena Mora and Adelaida R. del Castillo, 117–44 (Los Angeles: UCLA Chicano Studies Research Center Publications, 1980).

32. On the role that MASO played at ASU in Tempe, from 1968 to 1978, see Darius V. Echeverría, *Aztlán Arizona: Mexican American Educational Empowerment, 1968–1978* (Tucson: University of Arizona Press, 2014); quotation on p. 69.

33. Echeverría, *Aztlán Arizona*, 72–75.

34. Echeverría, *Aztlán Arizona*, 87–90.

35. For a history of defending and organizing Mexican-immigrant and Mexican American workers in the early 1900s, see Chacón, *Radicals in the Barrio*, esp. 320–84.

36. Jimmy Patino, *Raza Si, Migra No: Chicano Movement Struggles for Immigrant Rights in San Diego* (Durham: University of North Carolina Press, 2018).

37. García, *Memories of Chicano History*, 288–95.

38. García, *Memories of Chicano History*, 297–308.

39. García, *Memories of Chicano History*, 308–35. On the rise and fall of CASA in Los Angeles during the 1970s, see Ernie Chávez, *Mi Raza Primero! Nationalism, Identity, and Insurgency in the Chicano Movement in Los Angeles, 1966–1978* (Berkeley: University of California Press, 2002), chap. 5.

40. Patino, *Raza Si, Migra No*.

41. For an overview of the field of labor history in the early 1980s, see *The State of Chicano Research in Family, Labor, and Migration Studies: Proceedings of the First Stanford Symposium on Chicano Research and Public Policy*, ed. Armando Valdez, Albert Camarillo, and Tomás Almaguer (Stanford, CA: Stanford Research Center, 1983).

42. Oropeza, *Raza Si! Guerra No*.

43. "Chicano Moratorium: A Question of Freedom," YouTube, February 17, 2010, https://www.youtube.com/watch?v=famNeiosTVk.

44. For additional information on the opposition to the war in Vietnam, see George Mariscal, *Aztlán and Viet Nam: Chicano and Chicana Experiences of the War* (Berkeley: University of California Press, 1999); Armando Morales, *Ando sangrando* (Los Angeles, CA: Perspectiva Publications, 1972).

45. García, *United We Win*.

46. On the struggle against racism and for ethnic studies and bilingual education in the elementary grades, see Carlos E. Cortés, *The Making—and Remaking—of a Multiculturalist* (New York: Teacher's College Press, 2002), and Guadalupe San Miguel Jr., *Contested Policy: The Rise and Fall of Federal Bilingual Education in the United States, 1960–2001* (Denton: University of North Texas Press, 2004). For an excellent overview of the struggle for Chicano studies, see Rodolfo Acuña, *The Making of Chicano Studies: In the Trenches of Academe* (New Brunswick, NJ: Rutgers University Press, 2011).

47. Chicana activists also supported ongoing community struggles. Some of the best known were the UFW grape and lettuce boycotts, the strike by Farah workers in Texas, the desegregation of public education in Texas, and the struggle for equal financing of the public schools. For an excellent historical overview of Chicana involvement in the Chicano Movement see Vicki L. Ruiz, *From Out of the Shadows* (New York: Oxford University Press, 1998), 99–126.

48. For examples of two southwestern states engaged in struggles to promote ethnic studies during the years after 2010, see Augustine F. Romero, "At War with

the State in Order to Save the Lives of Our Children: The Battle to Save Ethnic Studies in Arizona," *Black Scholar* 40, no. 4 (2010); Aamena Ahmed, "SBOE [State Board of Education] Opts for Compromise on Mexican-American Studies," *Texas Tribune*, April 6, 2014, https://www.texastribune.org/2014/04/08 /activists-support-mexican-american-studies-class-a/; Mary Tuma, "SBOE Passes Mexican-American Studies, but Whitewashes the Name," *Austin Chronicle*, April 13, 2018, https://www.austinchronicle.com/daily/news/2018 -04-13/sboe-passes-mexican-american-studies-but-whitewashes-the-name/.

49. Ernie Chávez argued that one of the reasons for the demise of the Chicano Movement was activists' failure to consider the heterogeneous nature of the community they were organizing. Activists had a narrow definition of nationalism and tried to organize the complex community on the basis of one limited ideology. Chávez, *Mi Raza Primero*.

50. Oropeza, *Raza Si! Guerra No!*

51. García, *United We Win*; Marisela R. Chávez, "We Lived and Breathed and Worked the Movement": The Contradictions and Rewards of Chicana/ Mexicana Activism in el Centro de Acción Social Autónomo–Hermandad General de Trabajadores (CASA-HGT), Los Angeles, 1975–1978," in *Las Obreras: Chicana Politics of Work and Family*, ed. Vicki L. Ruiz (Los Angeles: UCLA Chicano Studies Research Center Publications, 1993); and Patricia Hernández, "Lives of Chicana Activists: The Chicano Student Movement (A Case Study)," in *Mexican Women in the United States: Struggles Past and Present*, ed. Magdalena Mora and Adelaida R. del Castillo (Los Angeles: UCLA Chicano Studies Research Center Publications, 1980), 7–16.

52. Muñoz, *Youth, Identity, Power*, 91–95. In the other case, the SWP and CASA competed for organizational hegemony over the issue of immigration in Texas in 1978. José Ángel Gutiérrez, in charge of the conference, eventually allowed the SWP to gain significant influence over this issue. See Richard A. García, "The Chicano Movement and the Mexican American Community," *Socialist Review* 8, nos. 40–41 (1978): 72–78.

53. See García, *Chicano Movement*, for additional case studies of factionalism, conflict, and schisms in student organizations. On MEChA see Gustavo Licón, "The Ideological Struggle for Chicana/o Unity and Power: A Short History of California MEChA," in García, *Chicano Movement*, 151–72. On moderate versus radical leaders of student groups in East Los Angeles see Marisol Moreno, "Understanding the Role of Conflict, Factionalism, and Schism in the Development of the Chicano Student Movement: The Mexican American Student Association and La Vida Nueva at East Los Angeles College, 1967–1969," in García, *Chicano Movement*, 173–200. On Brown Berets see Chávez, *Mi Raza Primero!* For the ways in which tensions and conflicts affected Chicano organizations in Crystal City and Houston see Navarro, *Cristal Experiment*, and San Miguel, *Brown, Not White*.

54. Maylei Blackwell, "Contested Histories: Las Hijas de Cuauhtémoc, Chicana Feminisms, and Print Culture in the Chicano Movement, 1968–1973," in *Chicana Feminisms: A Critical Reader*, ed. Gabriela F. Arredondo et al. (Durham, NC: Duke University Press, 2003).

55. Blackwell, *Chicana Power*.

56. García, *United We Win*. On party divisions in California, see Muñoz, *Youth, Identity, Power*, 90–91. For an overview of La Raza Unida Party and its tensions in Los Angeles, see Chávez, *Mi Raza Primero!*

57. For the role state repression played in suppressing the Chicano Movement see, for example, José Ángel Gutiérrez, *The Eagle Has Eyes: The FBI Surveillance of César Estrada Chávez of the United Farmworkers Union of America, 1965–1975* (East Lansing: Michigan State University Press, 2019), and Gutiérrez, *Tracking King Tiger: Reies López Tijerina and the FBI* (East Lansing: Michigan State University Press, 2019).

58. For an example of the diverse roles that Mexican American women played in the UFW, see Margaret Rose, "Traditional and Nontraditional Patterns of Female Activism in the United Farm Workers of America, 1962–1980," *Frontiers* 11, no. 1 (1990). For an example of the different roles Mexican American women played in two community-based organizations in Los Angeles, see Mary Pardo, "Mexican American Women Grassroots Community Activists: Mothers of East Los Angeles," *Frontiers* 12, no. 1 (1990). On the role of women in the MAEC in Houston, TX, see San Miguel, *Brown Not White*.

59. Vicki Ruiz notes that Chicana feminists were both inspired and frustrated by the sexism found within Chicano Movement organizations. Ruiz, *From Out of the Shadows*, 114–17.

60. Blackwell, *Chicana Power*, 62–63, 64.

61. Blackwell, *Chicana Power*, 65.

62. Anna NietoGomez and Adelaida del Castillo served as the first editors of *Encuentro Femenil*. Martha Cotera, *Profile of the Mexican American Woman* (Austin, TX: National Educational Laboratory, 1976), 164–65. For more information on their activities see Blackwell, *Chicana Power*, 65.

63. Rose, "Traditional and Nontraditional Patterns," 26–32.

64. Chávez, "We Lived and Breathed and Worked the Movement."

65. Dionne Espinoza, "'Revolutionary Sisters': Women's Solidarity and Collective Identification among Chicana Brown Berets in East Los Angeles, 1967–1970," *Aztlán* 26, no. 1 (2001).

66. Dionne Espinoza, "'The Partido Belongs to Those Who Will Work for It': Chicana Organizing and Leadership in the Texas Raza Unida Party, 1970–1990," *Aztlán* 36, no. 1 (2011).

67. San Miguel, *Brown, Not White*, 205.

68. San Miguel, *Brown, Not White*, 205. Women activists in Houston, I might add, were not explicitly feminist in orientation nor were they loyalists.

Feminists challenged male authority within the Chicano Movement, made decisions independent of men, and emphasized issues that were pertinent to women. Loyalists supported Chicano leaders and argued that "the gavacho, not the macho," was the central issue in the Chicano movement. The Houston women were in a third category of feminism that the historian Vicki Ruiz called "the Adelita" or "soldadera" perspective. The historical view of Adelita, an image born during the Mexican Revolution beginning in 1910, was of a strong, courageous woman fighting beside her man and caring for his needs. This image, argued Ruiz, embodied a conflicted middle ground between the two major factions of Chicana activists during the early 1970s—the feminists and the loyalists. Those with an Adelita mentality "could be fiercely independent, yet strongly male-identified." Ruiz, *From Out of the Shadows*, 111. Las mujeres in Houston displayed these characteristics. They identified with the male leaders, yet they took independent action in conjunction with other activists.

69. Women organized conferences, symposia, and rap sessions aimed at analyzing and proposing solutions to their specific problems. Additionally, they discussed types of organizations that could address their demands. García, *Chicana Feminist Thought*, 139.

70. For an overview of this struggle and a review of a documentary on the issue entitled *No más bebés por vida*, see Renee Tajima-Peña, "Más bebés?": An Investigation of the Sterilization of Mexican-American Women at Los Angeles County–USC Medical Center during the 1960s and '70s," Scholar & Feminist Online, http://sfonline.barnard.edu/life-un-ltd-feminism-bioscience-race/mas-bebes-an-investigation-of-the-sterilization-of-mexican-american-women-at-los-angeles-county-usc-medical-center-during-the-1960s-and-70s. See also Virginia Espino, "Women Sterilized as They Give Birth: Forced Sterilization and the Chicana Resistance in the 1970s," In *Las Obreras: Chicana Politics of Work and Family*, ed. Vicki L. Ruiz and Chon Noriega (Los Angeles: UCLA Chicano Studies Research Center Publications, 2000).

71. Daniela Jiménez, "'Informed (but Uneducated) Consent': Chicanas against Sterilization Abuse in California" (bachelor's thesis, Lewis and Clark College, May 2014), 6, https://watzek.lclark.edu/seniorprojects/files/original/b5d66752fdec4adb4ae8039ae889bc8f.pdf.

72. Clemencia Martínez, "Welfare Families Face Forced Labor," *La Raza* 1 (January 1972); Mary Tullos and Dolores Hernández, "Talmadge Amendment: Welfare Continues to Exploit the Poor," *La Raza* 1 (January 1972); Anna NietoGomez, "Madres por la Justicia," *Encuentro Femenil* 1 (Spring 1973); Alicia Escalante, "A Letter from the Chicana Welfare Rights Organization," *Encuentro Femenil* 1 (1973); Kathy Flores, "Chicano Attitudes toward Birth Control," *Imágenes de la Chicana* 1 (1974); Beverly Padilla, "Chicanas and Abortion," in García, *Chicana Feminist Thought*; Renne Mares, "La Pinta:

The Myth of Rehabilitation," *Encuentro Femenil* 1 (1974); Josie Madrid et al., "Chicanas in Prison," *Regeneración* 2 (1973): 53–54.

73. For an excellent perspective on the many ways in which Chicanas were involved in the Chicano Movement throughout the country during the 1960s and 1970s see Dionne Espinoza, et al., eds., *Chicana Movidas: New Narratives of Activism and Feminism in the Movement Era* (Austin: University of Texas Press, 2018).

74. Anna NietoGomez, "The Chicana—Perspectives for Education," and "CCHE Conference," both in García, *Chicana Feminist Thought*; Cynthia Orozco, "Sexism in Chicano Studies and in the Community," in *Chicana Voices: Intersections of Class, Race, and Gender,* ed. Teresa Cordova et al. (Albuquerque: University of New Mexico Press, 1993). Vicki Ruiz notes that Chicana feminists operated academic programs and, in 1982, established Mujeres Activas en Letras y Cambio Social (MALCS), an academic organization aimed at promoting feminism and activist scholarship. Ruiz, *From Out of the Shadows*, 123.

75. Sánchez, "Walkout Cabrones!"; Navarro, *Mexican American Youth Organization*, 115–48; San Miguel, "Beginning to Rumble"; Guajardo and Guajardo, "Impact of Brown on the Brown of South Texas"; *Chicano! The History of the Mexican American Civil Rights Movement,* episode 3: "Taking Back the Schools," PBS, 1996; Muñoz, "Politics of Protest and Chicano Liberation"; Myron Leslie Puckett, "Protest Politics in Education: A Case Study in the Los Angeles City School System" (PhD diss., Claremont Graduate School and University Center, 1971); Henry Joseph Gutiérrez, "The Chicano Education Rights Movement and School Desegregation: Los Angeles, 1962–1970" (PhD diss., University of California, Irvine, 1990); Delgado Bernal, "Chicana School Resistance"; García and Castro, *Blowout!*

76. Matt S. Meier and Feliciano Ribera, *Mexican Americans/American Mexicans: From Conquistadors to Chicanos* (San Francisco, CA: Hill and Wang, 1994), 235.

77. On the struggle for culturally relevant education, see the writings of José A. Cárdenas, one of the most passionate advocates of this cause. Cárdenas, *Multicultural Education: A Generation of Advocacy* (Needham Heights, MA: Simon and Schuster Custom Publishing, 1995).

78. In *Mexican Americans/American Mexicans*, Meier and Ribera argue that this led to a "cultural renaissance" throughout the country (235).

79. For a historical analysis of one of the most important U.S. *teatro* groups, see Broyles-González, *Teatro Campesino*. Chicano art became more personal and less political over the years. See Ella María Díaz, *Flying under the Radar with the Royal Chicano Air Force: Mapping a Chicano/a Art History* (Austin: University of Texas Press, 2017).

80. Richard Griswold del Castillo and Arnoldo De León, *North to Aztlán: A History of Mexican Americans in the United States* (New York: Twayne, 1996),

140–47. For a more recent interpretation of the role culture played in the Chicano Movement, see Randy Ontiveros, *In the Spirit of a New People: The Cultural Politics of the Chicano Movement* (New York: New York University Press, 2013).

81. The band was founded by Freddie Sánchez. They had several national hits in the late 1960s and early 1970s, including "Viva Tirado," a jazzy soul-rock rendition of Gerald Wilson's original song about a bullfighter; the funky "Tell Her She's Lovely"; and a cover of Van Morrison's 1967 hit "Brown Eyed Girl." Their first hit, "Viva Tirado," did very well on Los Angeles radio and remained at number 1 for thirteen straight weeks. Original members of El Chicano were Bobby Espinosa, Freddie Sánchez, Mickey Lespron, André Baeza, and John De Luna. During the 1970s, new members Ersi Arvisu as lead singer, Rudy Regalado, Max Garduno, Danny Lamonte, Brian Magness, Jerry Salas, and Joe *Perreira* joined the group. "El Chicano," Wikimedia Foundation, February 1, 2021, https://en.wikipedia.org/wiki/El_Chicano.

82. La Rondalla Amerindia de Aztlán, "No nos movarán," from the album *Rolas de Aztlán,* YouTube, https://www.youtube.com/watch?v=Zqc5GI5cTLg.

83. For versions of "You soy chicano" available on YouTube, see The Royal Jesters, https://www.youtube.com/watch?v=VNIPhr1yhho, and Los Alvarados, https://www.youtube.com/watch?v=k-sDrWVWALw.

84. On politically conscious music during the Chicano Movement in California, see Jim McCarthy with Ron Sansoe, *Voices of Latin Rock: The People and Events That Created This Sound* (Milwaukee, WI: Hal Leonard, 2004); and David Reyes and Tom Waldman, *Land of a Thousand Dances: Chicano Rock 'n' Roll from Southern California* (Albuquerque: University of New Mexico Press, 1998), 103–34. For Texas developments see San Miguel, *Tejano Proud,* 60–91.

## CHAPTER 4

1. Frank P. Barajas, "Community and Measured Militancy: The Ventura County Community Service Organization, 1958–1968," *Southern California Quarterly* 96, no. 3 (2014). Barajas argues that CSO mobilized and unified the Mexican-origin community in Oxnard, California, during the 1950s. Through a strategy of measured militancy—a mixture of lobbying, advocacy, and on occasion direct action—it also gave the community a voice in local, state, and national policy.

2. For an example of the shift from radical ideology and tactics in the late 1960s to more accommodating actions several years later in one organization, see John R. Chávez, *Eastside Landmark: A History of the East Los Angeles Community Union, 1968–1993* (Stanford, CA: Stanford University Press, 1998).

3. Richard Griswold del Castillo and Arnoldo De León argue that the older generation of leaders in groups such as LULAC and AGIF responded to the

growing radicalism by using their connections in Congress to ensure that Mexican Americans benefited from the new social agenda. See Griswold del Castillo and De León, *North to Aztlán*, 135.

4. "History and Legacy of the Southwest Voter Registration Education Project," SVREP, https://www.svrep.org/history.

5. "History and Legacy of the Southwest Voter Registration Education Project." In addition, SVREP sponsors a training program called the Latino Academy. This academy prepares and educates youth and experienced activists to lead local voter registration projects.

6. Badillo, *MALDEF and the Evolution of Latino Civil Rights*, Research Reports, Notre Dame, IN: Institute for Latino Studies, University of Notre Dame, January 2005, 7–8.

7. MALDEF's other cause was language rights violations in education (*Serna v. Portales Municipal Schools* [1972]). During the 1980s and 1990s, it tackled national and transnational issues, especially the plight of undocumented immigrants. Badillo, *MALDEF and the Evolution of Latino Civil Rights*, 7–8.

8. Vilma Socorro Martínez interview, Voces Oral History Project, Moody College of Communication, University of Texas at Austin; "Vilma Socorro Martínez," Your Dictionary, https://biography.yourdictionary.com/vilma-socorro-martinez.

9. "Vilma Socorro Martínez."

10. Ávila rose quickly through the MALDEF ranks. As president and general counsel of the organization from 1982 to 1985, he played crucial roles in filing and successfully arguing countless voting rights cases. In 1973, for instance, MALDEF successfully argued *White v. Regester* before the U.S. Supreme Court, a case that resulted in the implementation of single-member districts. For decades, Latino and minority communities had been denied full access to the political system in Texas through at-large voting districts. MALDEF argued that this system was discriminatory and should be replaced with a fairer way of electing individuals to policymaking boards. Although *White v. Regester* was remanded in 1975, the Texas legislature was forced to develop a less discriminatory system for electing individuals to local offices. This case then served as a precedent for Texas county, city council, and school board districts. It also accelerated the growing trend of electing Latinas/os and minorities to local and county positions in Texas. *White v. Regester*, 412 U.S. 755, 93 S. Ct. 2332 (1973).

11. For an overview of Ávila's approach to voting rights litigation see "Access to the Political Process and the Development of Leadership: A Key to Future Social Cohesiveness," *La Raza Law Journal* 11 (1999–2000): 91–97.

12. Badillo, *MALDEF and the Evolution of Latino Civil Rights*, 9.

13. Ari Berman, "The Lost Promise of the Voting Rights Act, *Atlantic*, August 5, 2015, https://www.theatlantic.com/politics/archive/2015/08/give-us-the-ballot-expanding-the-voting-rights-act/399128/.

14. These voting rights lawsuits, initiated in many cases by MALDEF and assisted by SVREP, targeted two major barriers: at-large systems and gerrymandering. See Berman, "Lost Promise."

15. Nina Perales, Luis Figueroa, and Criselda G. Rivas, "Voting Rights in Texas: 1982–2006," *Review of Law and Social Justice* 17, no. 2 (2008), 717. The number had increased to 1,687 by 1996. See National Association of Latino Elected and Appointed Officials (NALEO), *A Profile of Latino Elected Officials in the United States and Their Progress since 1996* (Los Angeles, CA: NALEO Education Fund, 2007).

16. See "Edward R. Roybal, "Eligio 'Kika' de la Garza II," "Henry B. González," and "Manuel Luján Jr.," all in *Hispanic Americans in Congress, 1822–2012*, prepared under the direction of the Committee on House Administration by the Office of the Historian and the Office of the Clerk, U.S. House of Representatives (Washington, DC: Government Printing Office, 2013), https://www.govinfo.gov/content/pkg/GPO-CDOC-108hdoc225/pdf/GPO-CDOC-108hdoc225.pdf; Julie Leininger Pycior, "Henry B. González," in *Profiles in Power: Twentieth-Century Texans in Washington*, ed. Kenneth E. Hendrickson et al. (Austin: University of Texas Press, 1993.

17. "Herman Badillo" and "Baltasar Corrada del Río," both in *Hispanic Americans in Congress, 1822–2012*.

18. Garrine P. Laney, *The Voting Rights Act of 1965, As Amended: Its History and Current Issues* (Hauppauge, NY: Nova Science, 2008); Voting Rights Act of 1975, P.L. 94–73, 89 Stat. 400 (1975); Juan Sepúlveda, *The Life and Times of Willie Velásquez: su voto es su voz* (Houston, TX: Arte Público Press, 2003).

19. For a complete list, see Appointments to Federal Government Positions, October 1968, Vicente Ximenes Papers, LBJ Library, Austin, TX.

20. Ramírez, *Chicano in the White House*, 155–58. Ramírez quotes one of Salazar's critical articles titled "The Mexican Americans NEDA Much Better School System," *Los Angeles Times*, August 28, 1970. See Ramírez, footnote on 460.

21. Kaplowitz, *LULAC*.

22. Ramírez, *Chicano in the White House*, 145.

23. According to one report, the number of Spanish-speaking individuals appointed to or hired for high-ranking positions in thirty-four agencies and twelve departments (in the GS-13 and above salary grades) and the number of full-time presidential appointees doubled between 1970 and 1972. No names however are listed in the report. See Memorandum for the President from Ken Cole, August 29, 1972, Henry M. Ramírez Collection, Richard M. Nixon Presidential Library, Yorba Linda, CA.

24. Ramírez, *Chicano in the White House*, 147.

25. The following departments/agencies were ordered to establish affirmative action committees: Department of Labor, Department of Commerce, SBA,

Office of Economic Opportunity, HEW, HUD, Justice, Agriculture, Treasury, EEOC, and Civil Service Commission. Each committee was assigned a COSSA staff member to assist them in their efforts. See Spanish-Speaking American Task Force, Folder 120, Box 42, Henry M. Ramírez Collection, Nixon Library.

26. Memorandum for the President from Ken Cole, Ramírez Collection, Nixon Library. For Ramírez's interpretation of his role in these affirmative action efforts during the Nixon administration, see Ramírez, *Chicano in the White House*.

27. Meier and Ribera, *Mexican Americans/American Mexicans*, 259.

28. Acuña, *Occupied America*, 287.

29. Allsup, *American G.I. Forum*, 149.

30. Allsup, *American G.I. Forum*, 147–48.

31. "Frito Bandito," Wikimedia Foundation, updated April 14, 2021, https://en.wikipedia.org/wiki/Frito_Bandito.

32. Mexican American organizations were divided on the José Jiménez character. The National Hispanic Media Coalition actually endorsed it and invited Bill Dana to join its advisory board. "Biography," Official Website of Bill Dana, 2008, http://www.bill-dana.com/pages/biography.html.

33. See, e.g., Gastón Espinosa and Mario T. García, *Mexican American Religions: Spirituality, Activism, and Culture* (Durham, NC: Duke University Press, 2008); Mario T. García, *Católicos: Resistance and Affirmation in Chicano Catholic History* (Austin: University of Texas Press, 2008).

34. Mario T. García, *Chicano Liberation Theology: The Writings and Documents of Richard Cruz and Católicos por La Raza* (Dubuque, IA: Kendall Hunt, 2009).

35. Other priests, including Patricio Flores and Virgilio Elizondo, also were founding members. María Eva Flores, "PADRES," Handbook of Texas Online, May 1, 1995, https://www.tshaonline.org/handbook/entries/padres.

36. Flores, "PADRES"; Richard Edward Martínez, *PADRES: The National Chicano Priest Movement* (Austin: University of Texas Press, 2005).

37. Three women accused Sánchez of having sexual relations with them in the 1970s and 1980s when they were teenagers. "Former Archbishop Robert Sánchez Has Died," *Santa Fe New Mexican*, January 20, 2012, http://www.bishop-accountability.org/news2012/01_02/2012_01_20_SantaFeNewMexican_FormerArchbishop.htm.

38. Elaine Ayala, "San Antonio's Retired Archbishop Patrick Flores, First Mexican-American bishop in the U.S., Has Died," *My San Antonio*, January 9, 2017, https://www.mysanantonio.com/news/local/article/Retired-archbishop-Patrick-Flores-has-died-10845168.php; Catholic New Service, "Archbishop Patrick Flores, First Hispanic Bishop in U.S., Dies," *National Catholic Reporter,*

January 10, 2017, https://www.ncronline.org/news/people/archbishop-patrick-flores-first-hispanic-bishop-us-dies.

39. María Eva Flores, "Las Hermanas," Handbook of Texas Online, https://www.tshaonline.org/handbook/entries/las-hermanas. Also see Lara Medina, *Las Hermanas: Chicana/Latina Religious-Political Activism in the U.S. Catholic Church* (Philadelphia: Temple University Press, 2005).

40. Felipe Hinojosa, *Latino Mennonites: Civil Rights, Faith, and Evangelical Culture* (Baltimore: Johns Hopkins University Press, 2014).

41. Henry A. J. Ramos, *The American G.I. Forum: In Pursuit of the Dream, 1948–1983* (Houston, TX: Arte Público Press, 1998).

42. Espino, "Women Sterilized as They Give Birth"; Tajima-Peña, "Más Bebés"; Dwight Watson, "The Storm Clouds of Change: The Death of José Campos Torres and the Emergence of Triracial Politics in Houston, 1978–1980," in *Race and the Houston Police Department, 1930–1990: A Change Did Come* (College Station: Texas A&M University Press, 2005), 110–29; Taylor Davidson, "The Death of Joe Torres and the Continued Fight against Police Brutality," *Chicana Por Mi Raza*, http://chicanapormiraza.org/content/death-joe-torres-continued-fight-against-police-brutality; Moises Sandoval, *On the Move: A History of the Hispanic Church in the United States* (Maryknoll, NY: Orbis Books, 1990), 64–69, 127–30; David G. Gutiérrez, *Walls and Mirrors: Mexican Americans, Mexican Immigrants, and the Politics of Ethnicity* (Berkeley: University of California Press, 1995), 179–205.

43. Benjamin Márquez, *LULAC: The Evolution of a Mexican American Political Organization* (Austin: University of Texas Press, 1993), 74.

44. Ramos, *American G.I. Forum*, 116 18.

45. In the 1980s and 1990s, LULAC established several other leadership development programs for Hispanic high school students, an innovative literacy program for elementary students, and an intensive tutoring and counseling program for seventh and eighth graders. Its most visible program, however, was LNESC. By 2018 LNESC had assisted more than three million students, sent 140,000 to college, and awarded in excess of $8 million in scholarships to more than 12,000 students. "LULAC National Educational Service Centers," League of United Latin American Citizens, https://lulac.org/programs/education/centers/.

46. For an excellent brief history of the origins of CDCs in the 1960s, see Chávez, *Eastside Landmark*, 39–45. For general information on CDCs, see Lawrence F. Parachini, *A Political History of the Special Impact Program* (Cambridge, MA: Center for Community Economic Development, 1980).

47. For an overview of all these CDCs, see Chávez, *Eastside Landmark*, 137–65.

48. Chávez, *Eastside Landmark*, 77–106.

49. Chávez, *Eastside Landmark*, 223–51. "The TELACU Story," TELACU: 50 Years, 1968–2018, 2021, https://telacu.com/telacu-story/our-history/.

50. F. Arturo Rosales, "Chicanos Por La Causa (CPLC)," in *Latinas in the United States: A Historical Encyclopedia*, ed. Vicki L. Ruiz and Virginia Sánchez Korrol, 155 (Bloomington: Indiana University Press, 2006).

51. For more on the CPLC's radical activities in the schools and the community during the Chicano Movement years, see Echeverría, *Aztlán Arizona*.

52. Pete Dimas, ed., *Here We Stand: Chicanos Por La Causa and Arizona's Chicano/a Resurgence, 1968–1974* (Phoenix: Chicanos Por La Causa, 2019). See also "Chicanos Por La Causa, Dime quien eres," a documentary produced by PBS Arizona in 2018, available at www.CPLC.org/documentary.

53. "Our History," MAUC, https://www.mauc.org/about/.

54. Over the next several years Cortés organized additional faith-based organizations in Los Angeles, Houston, and other parts of the Southwest. These organizations eventually became part of the West/Southwest IAF network. These IAF chapters have improved public education, increased access to job training and decent jobs, and tackled other issues such as immigration, health care, and economic development. "Rutgers to Confer Four Honorary Degrees at 245th Commencement," *Rutgers Today*, April 5, 2011, https://www.rutgers.edu/news/rutgers-confer-four-honorary-degrees-245th-commencement.

55. "History," COPS/Metro, http://www.copsmetro.com/history.

56. For an overview of CSO's development in California, see Barajas, "Community and Measured Militancy."

57. On the large number of affiliates formed by the IAF, see "IAF Organizations in the United States," Industrial Areas Foundation, https://www.industrialareasfoundation.org/affiliates.

58. For an excellent discussion by Ernesto Cortés Jr. on his ideas about social change and community organizing see "Rules for Radicals in the 21st Century," YouTube, April 19, 2017, https://www.youtube.com/watch?v=JX_ry6V44E4&feature=youtu.be; see also Mary Beth Rogers, *Cold Anger: A Story of Faith and Power Politics* (Denton: University of North Texas Press, 2012).

59. The Metro Alliance, another IAF group, was formed in 1989. COPS and the Metro Alliance merged into a collective unit to expand educational and social opportunities for those living in the West and South Sides of San Antonio. For a brief history of these groups, see Lea Thompson, "COPS/Metro Alliance: 40 Years of Community Change," *San Antonio Report*, April 15, 2016, https://therivardreport.com/copsmetro-alliance-40-years-of-community-change/; and Roberto Vásquez, "The San Antonio COPS Revolution," LaRed Latina of the Intermountain Southwest, March 14, 2005, http://www.lared-latina.com/cops.htm.

60. "History," COPS/Metro.

61. "History," COPS/Metro; quotation from Vásquez, "San Antonio COPS Revolution."

62. Moises Sandoval, "The Decolonization of a City," *Alicia Patterson Foundation newsletter*, 1978, archived on the Way Back Machine at https://web.archive.org/web/20061002100025/http://aliciapatterson.org/APF001977/Sandoval/Sandoval04/Sandoval04.html.

63. Thompson, "COPS/Metro Alliance."

64. Vásquez, "San Antonio COPS Revolution," 4–5, quotation on p. 5.

65. Dimas, *Here We Stand*.

66. Sandra Ivette Enríquez, "El barrio unido jamás será vencido! Neighborhood Grassroots Activism and Community Preservation in El Paso, Texas" (PhD diss., University of Houston, 2016).

### CHAPTER 5

1. For an overview of the struggle against segregation in the 1960s and 1970s, see Guadalupe San Miguel Jr., *Chicana/o Struggles for Education: Activism in the Community* (College Station: Texas A&M University Press, 2013), 32–37.

2. For an excellent and detailed discussion of these lawsuits, see Richard R. Valencia, *Chicano Students and the Courts: The Mexican-American Legal Struggle for Educational Equality* (New York: New York University Press, 2008). See also San Miguel, *Chicana/o Struggles for Education*, 37–56.

3. Paul A. Sracic, San Antonio v. Rodríguez *and the Pursuit of Equal Education* (Lawrence: University Press of Kansas, 2006), 20–23, 152–53.

4. The emphasis of the OCR was on Mexican Americans, though the designation of national-origin minority groups also included Native Americans, Puerto Ricans, and Asian Americans. See Martin H. Gerry, "Cultural Freedom in the Schools: The Right of Mexican-American Children to Succeed," in *Mexican Americans and Educational Change*, ed. Alfredo Castañeda et al., 226–54 (New York: Arno Press, 1974). (In 1971, Gerry was a special assistant to the director of OCR).

5. Title VI, Civil Rights Act of 1964, 42 U.S.C. 2000d, https://www.dol.gov/oasam/regs/statutes/titlevi.htm.

6. J. Stanley Pottinger, Memorandum of May 25, 1970, to School Districts with More than Five Percent National Origin-Minority Group Children, Office for Civil Rights, Department of Health, Education, and Welfare, Washington, DC, 1970.

7. Specifically, school districts "must not assign national origin-minority group students to classes for the mentally retarded on the basis of criteria which essentially measure or evaluate English language skills; nor may school districts deny national origin-minority group children access to college preparatory course on a basis directly related to the failure of the school system to inculcate English language skills." Pottinger, Memorandum of May 25, 1970.

8. Pottinger, Memorandum of May 25, 1970.

9. Pottinger, Memorandum of May 25, 1970.

10. Memorandum from J. Stanley Pottinger, director, Office for Civil Rights, to Secretary of Department of Health, Education, and Welfare, n.d., p. 6, Stanley Pottinger Papers, Folder 239 (1) Box 18, Gerald D. Ford Presidential Library, Ann Arbor, MI.

11. Memorandum from Pottinger to secretary of HEW.

12. The taskforce had thirty-four members; sixteen were department staff personnel, seven of whom were Mexican American. Of the seventeen participants from outside the department, thirteen were Mexican Americans and one was Puerto Rican. In total, then, more than half the members were Mexican American. Among them were Dr. Alfredo Castañeda (University of California, Riverside); Dr. Edward de Avila (Bilingual Children's Television Project, Oakland, CA); Dr. Uvaldo Palomares (Institute for Personal Effectiveness in Children, San Diego, CA); Dr. Manuel Ramírez (University of California, Riverside); Felipe Montez (U.S. Commission on Civil Rights, Los Angeles); and Henry Casso (University of Massachusetts, Amherst). The list of members is contained in Appendix A of Memorandum from Pottinger to Secretary of HEW, p. 12.

13. The conference was titled The Identification of Discrimination and Denial of Services on the Basis of National Origin. For a summary of it, see James V. Gambone, "Bilingual Bicultural Educational Civil Rights: The May 25th Memorandum and Oppressive School Practices" (PhD diss., University of New Mexico, 1973); and Martin H. Gerry, "Cultural Myopia: The Need for a Corrective Lens," *Journal of School Psychology* 11, no. 4 (1973): 309.

14. Gambone, "Bilingual Bicultural Educational Civil Rights," 20, fn. 22. Gambone also notes that some participants criticized the conference for having limited representation from local community organizations, Native Americans, Puerto Ricans, and Asian Americans.

15. Among the components the group identified were the use of pluralistic norms, sociocultural background data to interpret test results, and adaptive behavior. The findings emphasized the necessity and nature of community involvement. Gerry, "Cultural Freedom in the Schools," 245; Gerry, "Cultural Myopia," 307–15.

16. Among the recommendations were the hiring of national-origin-minority teachers and staff; an attitude shift toward national-origin-minority children among school board members, school staff, and students; inclusion of minority history in the textbooks, and the establishment of bilingual and bicultural education "so that children will be proud of their language and their heritage." See A Summary of the Denver Conference—Identification of Discrimination

and Denial of Services on the Basis of National Origin, report sent to Elliot Richardson from Stan Pottinger, director of OCR [June 1970], quoted in Gambone, "Bilingual Bicultural Educational Civil Rights," 22.

17. In August 1970, Elliot Richardson, secretary of HEW, summarized the committee's recommendations in a letter to Senator Walter Mondale. The influence of Mexican American perspectives was apparent in his letter, which echoed many of their concerns. Richardson acknowledged the severe and long-term effects of segregation on national-origin-minority children and noted the variety of needs identified in the conference: (1) the need for ethnic or cultural diversity in the educational environment; and (2) the need for total institutional reposturing in order to incorporate, affirmatively recognize, and value the cultural environment of ethnic minority children so that the development of positive self-concept can be accelerated. He recognized a need for language programs that would introduce and develop English-language skills without demeaning or otherwise deprecating the child's home language and without presenting English as a more valued language. Elliot L. Richardson, secretary of HEW, to Senator Walter F. Mondale, Subcommittee on Education, August 3, 1970. Cited in Gerry, "Cultural Freedom in the Schools," 246–48.

18. Among the innovations Dr. Cárdenas and his team introduced were programs in "early childhood and bilingual education, parent and community involvement, staff development, staff differentiation, teacher aide development, special education, peer-tutoring, ethnic studies, and other areas." Blandina Cárdenas, "Defining Equal Access to Educational Opportunity for Mexican American Children: A Study of Three Civil Rights Actions Affecting Mexican American Students and the Development of a Conceptual Framework for Effecting Institutional Responsiveness to the Educational Needs of Mexican American Children" (EdD diss., University of Massachusetts, 1974), 63.

19. B. Cárdenas, "Defining Equal Access," 63.

20. J. Stanley Pottinger to Secretary of HEW, 13.

21. B. Cárdenas, "Defining Equal Access," 65.

22. The list of members can be found in an appendix to Memorandum from J. Stanley Pottinger to Secretary of HEW, Folder 239 (4), Box 18, Stanley Pottinger Papers, Ford Library.

23. Gambone, "Bilingual Bicultural Educational Civil Rights," 23.

24. Earles had been a teacher in that city's bilingual program since 1964 and had guided its evolution into one of the most successful programs in the country. For an overview see *The Invisible Minority*, Report of the NEA-Tucson Survey on the Teaching of Spanish to the Spanish-Speaking (Washington, DC: Department of Rural Education/NEA, 1966), 13–17.

25. Known as the Esperanza Model, this plan was created by Dr. Tomás Arciniega and implemented by Juan Aragón with Joe Ulibarrí, Mari-Luci

Jaramillo, and Jim Miller at the University of New Mexico. See Juan Aragón, "The Challenge to Biculturalism: Culturally Deficient Educators Teaching Culturally Different Children," in Castañeda et al., *Mexican Americans and Educational Change*, 258–67.

26. On the Follow Through model, see Manuel Ramírez III, "Bilingual Education as a Vehicle for Institutional Change," in Castañeda et al., *Mexican Americans and Educational Change*.

27. B. Cárdenas, "Defining Equal Access," 185.

28. Most attendees at this meeting also agreed that all children, not just national-origin-minority-group children, needed this type of program. The participation of Anglo-American children in these programs, in other words, was essential. Gerry, "Cultural Freedom in the Schools," 248.

29. B. Cárdenas, "Defining Equal Access," 66. The dates of these meetings come from Memorandum from Pottinger to Secretary of HEW, Appendix O, Pottinger Papers.

30. The committee members' critiques that additional national-origin-minority groups and community organizations should participate and their recognition of the complexity of school practices affecting the education of these children prodded the Office of Education to establish the Intra-departmental Advisory Committee on Bilingual Education in 1971. Gambone argues that the Office of Education was not interested in cooperating with the OCR but through some "clever political manipulations," the latter was able to nudge the "lethargic" Office of Education to act. Gambone, "Bilingual Bicultural Educational Civil Rights," fn. 24, 22. The mandate of the Intra-departmental Advisory Committee was to develop strategies for providing educational program assistance to school districts found not to be in compliance. See Gerry, "Cultural Freedom in the Schools," 246. Committee members were Juan Aragón, Manuel Carrillo, Henry Casso, Gilbert Chávez, Martin Gerry, Armando Rodríguez, and Blandina Cárdenas. See B. Cárdenas, "Defining Equal Access," 65.

31. For an overview of their participation in these efforts, see B. Cárdenas, "Defining Equal Access," 76–164.

32. For two examples of programs that educators of Mexican American children supported, see National Conference on Educational Opportunities for Mexican-Americans, April 25–26, 1968, Austin, TX. See also Charles B. Brussell, *Disadvantaged Mexican American Children and Early Educational Experience* (Austin, TX: Southwest Educational Development Corporation, 1968).

33. Governor's Committee on Public School Education, *The Challenge and the Chance*, vol. 2, *Public Education in Texas–Program Evaluation* (Austin: Governor's Committee, 1969).

34. For a sampling of the literature on meeting the linguistic, cultural, and aca-demic needs of Mexican Americans, see Henry Sioux Johnson and William J. Hernández-M., *Educating the Mexican Americans* (Valley Forge, PA: Judson Press, 1970); Earl J. Ogletree and David Garcia, eds., *Education of the Spanish-Speaking Urban Child* (Springfield, IL: Charles C. Thomas, 1975); and Castañeda et al., *Mexican Americans and Educational Change*.

35. See, for instance, Carlos E. Cortés, "Revising the 'All-American Soul Course': A Bicultural Avenue to Educational Reform," In Castañeda et al., *Mexican Americans and Educational Change*.

36. *Invisible Minority*, 1966.

37. San Miguel, *Contested Policy*, 5–25; Cortés, "Revising the 'All-American Soul Course'"; Ramírez, "Bilingual Education as a Vehicle for Institutional Change," 390–91.

38. Bilingual education was continually buffeted by a variety of factors, such as special interest groups, changing political environments, government officials, and economic recessions. Of particular concern was the power that federal agencies, the federal courts, national minorities, and special interest groups had over its development. For an overview see San Miguel, *Contested Policy*.

39. Maritza de la Trinidad, "Mexican Americans and the Push for Culturally Rel-evant Education: The Bilingual Education Movement in Tucson, 1958–1969," *History of Education* 44, no. 3 (2015).

40. Elizabeth Quiroz González, "The Education and Public Career of Maria L. Urquides: A Case Study of a Mexican American Community Leader" (EdD diss., University of Arizona, 1986), 63.

41. "National Defense Education Act of 1958, P.L. 85-864," Discover U.S. Gov-ernment Information, https://www.govinfo.gov/content/pkg/STATUTE-72/pdf/STATUTE-72-Pg1580.pdf.

42. González, "Education and Public Career of Maria L. Urquides," 63.

43. In early January 1967, on introducing the bill in the U.S. Senate, Yarbor-ough stated, "The time for action is upon us. Mexican Americans have not achieved equality of opportunity in this country." He described them as vic-tims of "the cruelest form of discrimination" in the schools. He further added, "English only policies, no-Spanish speaking rules, and cultural degradation have caused great psychological harm to these children and contributed to their poor performance in school and high dropout rates. Bilingual education can overcome many of these problems and improve their academic achieve-ment." See Ralph Yarborough, "Two Proposals for a Better Way of Life for Mexican Americans in the Southwest," *Congressional Record*, January 17, 1967, 599–600.

44. The other three individuals contributing to the formulation of the bilingual bill were Monroe Sweetland, Alan Mandel, and Gene Godley. Sweetland was

the West Coast representative for the NEA. Mandel and Godley were Yarborough's assistants. Gilbert Sánchez, "An Analysis of the Bilingual Education Act, 1967–1968" (PhD diss., University of Massachusetts, 1973).

45. Three Mexican American legislators—Henry B. González (D-TX), Kika de la Garza (D-TX), and Joseph Montoya (D-NM)—either did not support the bill or believed it was unnecessary. According to Gilbert Sánchez, Roybal was the only Mexican American to support its passage. Sánchez, "Analysis of the Bilingual Education Act," 94. Roybal worked closely with four members of Congress leading the effort to pass the bill: James Scheuer (D-NY) and Roman C. Pucinski, (D-Ill), respectively, member and chair of the House General Subcommittee on Education; Augustus Hawkins (D-CA), member of the House Committee on Education and Labor; and Senator Ralph Yarborough (D-TX). Sánchez, "Analysis of the Bilingual Education Act," 85–97.

46. On Bernal's views regarding bilingual education and the need for state involvement in its support, see Joseph Bernal, "The Role of the State," in Sioux Johnson and Hernández-M., *Educating the Mexican Americans*, 363–68.

47. Sánchez, "Analysis of the Bilingual Education Act," 26–27.

48. For the key roles Bernal and Truan played in promoting bilingual education in Texas, see San Miguel, *Let All of Them Take Heed*, 192–213. See also Vega, *Education, Politics, and Bilingualism in Texas*.

49. Although Urquides believed that students needed to master English, she did not think they needed to do so at the expense of their native language. She believed that if children were taught to be proud of who they were, they could be successful in school. To that end, the curriculum and teaching methods needed to be culturally and linguistically relevant for Mexican American students. De la Trinidad, "Mexican Americans and the Push for Culturally Relevant Education," 325.

50. De la Trinidad, "Mexican Americans and the Push for Culturally Relevant Education," 63–65, 325–27.

51. On the prohibition of Spanish and promotion of English-only policies in the schools, see San Miguel, *Let All of Them Take Heed*; Gilbert G. González, *Chicano Education in the Era of Segregation* (Philadelphia: Balch Institute Press, 1990); Carlos Kevin Blanton, *The Strange Career of Bilingual Education in Texas, 1836–1981* (College Station: Texas A&M University Press, 2004); Erlinda González-Berry, "Which Language Will Our Children Speak? The Spanish Language and Public Education Policy in New Mexico, 1890–1930," in *The Contested Homeland: A Chicano History of New Mexico*, ed. Erlinda González-Berry and David R. Maciel (Albuquerque: University of New Mexico Press, 2000).

52. Joseph A. Rodríguez and Vicki L. Ruiz, "At Loose Ends: Twentieth-Century Latinos in Current United States History Textbooks," *Journal of American History* 86, no. 4 (2000), 1689.

53. De la Trinidad, "Mexican Americans and the Push for Culturally Relevant Education," 329.
54. González, "Education and Public Career of Maria L. Urquides."
55. Ramírez, *Chicano in the White House*, 294–300.
56. Ramírez, *Chicano in the White House*, 339–62.
57. Armando Rodríguez, *From the Barrio to Washington: An Educator's Journey* (Albuquerque: University of New Mexico Press, 2007), 57–58.
58. Rodríguez, *From the Barrio to Washington*, 59–63.
59. Rodríguez, *From the Barrio to Washington*, 65–75.
60. Nick E. Garza Sr, obituary, Legacy.com, February 16, 2008, https://www.legacy.com/obituaries/sanantonio/obituary.aspx?page=lifestory&pid=103574272.
61. "Statement of Nick Garza, Principal, J. T. Brackenridge Elementary School, San Antonio, Texas," Hearings before the Special Subcommittee on Bilingual Education of the Committee on Labor and Public Welfare, United States Senate, 90th Cong., 1st. Sess. (Washington, DC: Government Printing Office, 1967).
62. José A. Cárdenas, "Edgewood Independent School District, Experimental Schools Education Plan," 1972, Folder 26, Box 1, José A. Cárdenas Papers, Benson Latin American Collection, University of Texas at Austin.
63. Cárdenas, "Edgewood Independent School District," 3.
64. For a discussion of this theory and its components, see José A. Cárdenas and Blandina Cárdenas, "The Theory of Incompatibilities," in *Multicultural Education: A Generation of Advocacy*, ed. José A. Cárdenas, 20–34 (Needham Heights, MA: Simon and Schuster Custom Publishing, 1995).

## CONCLUSION

1. García, *Mexican Americans*.
2. Rhinehart and Kreneck, "Minimum Wage March of 1966," 27–33.
3. For several photos of his arrest, see San Miguel, *Chicana/o Struggles for Education*, 26–27.
4. For one example of Rodríguez's support of radicalism in the community, see "Speak Up Chicano."
5. On the Del Rio protest, see Homer Bigart, "Mexican-Americans Stage Protest March," *New York Times*, March 31, 1969, https://www.nytimes.com/1969/03/31/archives/mexicanamericans-stage-protest-march-in-texas.html.
6. Benjamin Márquez notes that in addition to rejecting radicalism, many LULAC members also rejected liberal or progressive tendencies within the organization and the increased assertiveness of its leaders. The organization was in decline during these years, as indicated by complaints over higher dues, missed publications of *LULAC News*, and declining membership. Márquez, *LULAC*, 68–69.

7. Márquez, *LULAC*, 64–65, quotation on 67.

8. Bonilla served as president of LULAC for two years. García, *Chicanismo*, fn. 77, 153.

9. David Montejano, *Quixote's Soldiers: A Local History of the Chicano Movement, 1966–1981* (Austin: University of Texas Press, 2010), 83–87.

10. Montejano, *Quixote's Soldiers*, 83–87.

11. Montejano, *Quixote's Soldiers*, 83–87.

12. Montejano, *Quixote's Soldiers*, 83–87.

13. Frank Barajas has defined measured militancy as the combined use of lobbying, advocacy, and occasional direct action tactics to achieve moderate change. See Barajas, "Community and Measured Militancy." For an example of the shift from radical ideology and tactics in the late 1960s to more accommodating actions several years later in one organization, see Chávez, *Eastside Landmark*.

# Bibliography

## ARCHIVAL SOURCES

Cabinet Committee on Opportunities for Spanish-Speaking People. Richard Nixon Presidential Library. Yorba Linda, CA.

Chicana Por Mi Raza Digital Memory Project and Archive. chicanapormiraza.org/.

COPS/Metro Alliance Records. Special Collections. University of Texas at San Antonio Libraries.

Hector P. García Collection. Mary and Jeff Bell Library. Texas A&M University–Corpus Christi.

Inter-Agency Committee on Mexican-American Affairs. LBJ Presidential Library, Austin, TX.

Irvine Sprague Papers. LBJ Presidential Library, Austin, TX

J. Stanley Pottinger Papers. Gerald R. Ford Presidential Library. Ann Arbor, MI.

Joe Bernal Papers. Benson Latin American Collection. University of Texas at Austin.

José A. Cárdenas Papers and Records of the Intercultural Development Research Association (IDRA). Benson Latin American Collection. University of Texas at Austin.

Martha Cotera Papers. Benson Latin American Collection. University of Texas at Austin.

Mexican American Oral History Collection. Houston Metropolitan Research Center (HMRC). Houston Public Library, Houston, TX.

National Council of La Raza Records. Special Collections. Stanford University. Stanford, CA

Oral History Project—Civil Rights in Black and Brown. Texas Christian University. Ft. Worth, TX.

Vicente Ximenes Papers, LBJ Presidential Library, Austin, TX.

Voces Oral History Project, University of Texas at Austin.

## GOVERNMENT DOCUMENTS

Cabinet Committee on Opportunities for the Spanish-Speaking People. P.L. 91-81, 83 Stat. 838 (1969). See also 42 U.S.C., § 4301 (Supp. V, 1970).

Coleman, James S. *Equality of Educational Opportunity.* Washington, DC: Government Printing Office, 1966.

Establish an Inter-Agency Committee on Mexican-American Affairs: Hearings before the Subcommittee on Executive Reorganization of the Committee on Government Operations. United States Senate, 91st Cong., 740 (1969).

Establishing the Cabinet Committee on Opportunities for Spanish-Speaking People: Hearings before a Subcommittee of the Committee on Government Operations. House of Representatives, 91st Cong. 18 (1969).

Garza, Nick. Statement of Nick Garza, Principal, J. T. Brackenridge Elementary School, San Antonio, Texas. Hearings before the Special Subcommittee on Bilingual Education of the Committee on Labor and Public Welfare. United States Senate, 90th Cong., 1st Sess., S. 428, Parts 1 and 2.

Governor's Committee on Public School Education. *The Challenge and the Chance*, vol. 2, *Public Education in Texas–Program Evaluation* (Austin, TX: Office of the Governor, 1969).

*Hispanic Americans in Congress, 1822–2012*. Prepared under the direction of the Committee on House Administration by the Office of the Historian and the Office of the Clerk, U.S. House of Representatives. Washington, DC: Government Printing Office, 2013.

*The Mexican American, A New Focus on Opportunity: Testimony Presented at the Cabinet Committee Hearings on Mexican American Affairs, El Paso, Texas, October 26–28, 1967.* Washington, DC: Inter-Agency Committee on Mexican-American Affairs, 1968.

National Defense Education Act. P.L. 85-864, 72 Stat. September 2, 1958.

Navarro Uranga, Susan. "The Study of Mexican American Education in the Southwest: Implications of Research by the Civil Rights Commission." Washington, DC: U.S. Commission on Civil Rights, 1972. ERIC document 070 545 RC 006 617.

Nixon, Richard. "Statement on Signing the Bill Establishing the Cabinet Committee on Opportunities for Spanish-Speaking People." December 31, 1969. The American Presidency Project, https://www.presidency.ucsb.edu/documents/statement-signing-the-bill-establishing-the-cabinet-committee-opportunities-for-spanish.

Pottinger, J. Stanley. Memorandum of May 25, 1970, to School Districts with More than Five Percent National Origin-Minority Group Children, Office for Civil Rights, Department of Health, Education and Welfare, Washington, DC, 1970.

Title VI, Civil Rights Act of 1964, 42 U.S.C. 2000d. https://www.dol.gov/oasam/regs/statutes/titlevi.htm.

U.S. Commission on Civil Rights. *Ethnic Isolation of Mexican Americans in the Public Schools of the Southwest.* Report I of the Mexican American Education Study. Washington, DC: Government Printing Office. April 1971.

————. *The Excluded Student*. Report III of the Mexican American Education Study. Washington, DC: Government Printing Office, 1972.

————. *Hearings before the U.S. Commission on Civil Rights, Dec. 9–14, 1968, San Antonio*. Washington, DC: Government Printing Office, 1969.

————. *Mexican American Education in Texas: A Function of Wealth*. Report IV of the Mexican American Education Study. Washington, DC: Government Printing Office, 1972.

————. *Teachers and Students—Differences in Teacher Interaction with Mexican American and Anglo Students*. Report V of the Mexican American Education Study. Washington, DC: Government Printing Office, March 1973.

————. *Toward Quality Education for Mexican American Children*. Report VI of the Mexican American Education Study. Washington, DC: Government Printing Office, January 1974.

————. *The Unfinished Education—Educational Practices Affecting Mexican Americans in the Southwest*. Report II of the Mexican American Education Study.. Washington, DC: Government Printing Office, May 1972.

**SECONDARY SOURCES**

Acuña, Rodolfo F. *The Making of Chicano Studies: In the Trenches of Academe*. New Brunswick, NJ: Rutgers University Press, 2011.

————. *Occupied America: A History of Chicanos*. 5th ed. New York: Pearson, 2004.

Alamillo, José M. *Making Lemonade Out of Lemons: Mexican American Labor and Leisure in a California Town, 1880–1960*. Chicago: University of Illinois Press, 2006.

Allsup, Carl. *The American G.I. Forum: Origins and Evolution*. Austin: University of Texas Press, 1982.

Anderson, Terry H. *The Movement and the Sixties: Protest in America from Greensboro to Wounded Knee*. New York: Oxford University Press, 1995.

Ávila, Joaquín G. "Access to the Political Process and the Development of Leadership: A Key to Future Social Cohesiveness." *La Raza Law Journal* 11 (1999–2000): 91–97.

Badillo, David A. *MALDEF and the Evolution of Latino Civil Rights*. Research Reports. Notre Dame, IN: Institute for Latino Studies, University of Notre Dame, January 2005.

Barajas, Frank P. "Community and Measured Militancy: The Ventura County Community Service Organization, 1958–1968." *Southern California Quarterly* 96, no. 3 (2014): 313–49.

Barrera, Baldemar James. "Edcouch-Elsa High School Walkout: Chicano Student Activism in a South Texas Community." Master's thesis, University of Texas at El Paso, 2001.

———. "The 1968 San Antonio School Walkouts: The Beginning of the Chicano Student Movement in South Texas." *Journal of South Texas* 21, no. 1 (2008): 39–61.

———. "'We Want Better Education!': The Chicano Student Movement for Educational Reform in South Texas, 1968–1970." PhD diss., University of New Mexico, 2007.

Blackwell, Maylei. *Chicana Power: Contested Histories of Feminism in the Chicano Movement.* Austin: University of Texas Press, 2011.

———. "Contested Histories: Las Hijas de Cuauhtémoc, Chicana Feminisms, and Print Culture in the Chicano Movement, 1968–1973." In *Chicana Feminisms: A Critical Reader,* edited by Gabriela F. Arredondo, Aida Hurtado, Norma Klahn, Olga Nájera-Ramírez, and Patricia Zavella, 59–89. Durham, NC: Duke University Press, 2003.

Blanton, Carlos Kevin. "George I. Sánchez, Ideology, and Whiteness in the Making of the Mexican American Civil Rights Movement, 1930–1960." *Journal of Southern History* 72, no. 3 (2006): 569–604.

———. *The Strange Career of Bilingual Education in Texas, 1836–1981.* College Station: Texas A&M University Press, 2004.

Blawis, Patricia Bell. *Tijerina and the Land Grants: Mexican Americans in Struggle for Their Heritage.* New York: International Publishers, 1971.

Briegel, Kaye. "Chicano Student Militancy: The Los Angeles High School Strike of 1968." In *An Awakened Minority: The Mexican Americans,* edited by Manuel P. Servin, 215–25. New York: Macmillan, 1974.

Broyles-González, Yolanda. *El Teatro Campesino: Theater in the Chicano Movement.* Austin: University of Texas Press, 1994.

Brussell, Charles B. *Disadvantaged Mexican American Children and Early Educational Experience.* Austin, TX: Southwest Educational Development Corporation, 1968.

Cárdenas, Blandina. "Defining Equal Access to Educational Opportunity for Mexican American Children: A Study of Three Civil Rights Actions Affecting Mexican American Students and the Development of a Conceptual Framework for Effecting Institutional Responsiveness to the Educational Needs of Mexican American Children." EdD diss., University of Massachusetts, 1974.

Cárdenas, José A. *Multicultural Education: A Generation of Advocacy.* Needham Heights, MA: Simon and Schuster Custom Publishing, 1995.

Castañeda, Alfredo, et al., eds. *Mexican Americans and Educational Change.* New York: Arno Press, 1974.

"CCHE Conference." In *Chicana Feminist Thought: The Basic Historical Writings,* edited by Alma M. García, ed., 164–65. New York: Routledge, 1997.

Chacón, Justin Akers. *Radicals in the Barrio: Magonistas, Socialists, Wobblies, and Communists in the Mexican American Working Class.* Chicago: Haymarket Books, 2018.

Chávez, Ernie. *Mi raza primero! Nationalism, Identity, and Insurgency in the Chicano Movement in Los Angeles, 1966–1978.* Berkeley: University of California Press, 2002.

Chávez, John R. *Eastside Landmark: A History of the East Los Angeles Community Union, 1968–1993.* Stanford, CA: Stanford University Press, 1998.

Chávez, Marisela R. "We Lived and Breathed and Worked the Movement": The Contradictions and Rewards of Chicana/Mexicana Activism in el Centro de Acción Social Autónomo–Hermandad General de Trabajadores (CASA-HGT), Los Angeles, 1975–1978." In *Las Obreras: Chicana Politics of Work and Family,* edited by Vicki L. Ruiz, 83–105. Los Angeles: UCLA Chicano Studies Research Center Publications, 1993.

Chicano Coordinating Council on Higher Education. *El Plan de Santa Barbara.* Santa Barbara, CA: La Causa Publications, 1970.

Cortés, Carlos E. *The Making—and Remaking—of a Multiculturalist.* New York: Teacher's College Press, 2002.

Cotera, Martha. *Profile of the Mexican American Woman.* Austin, TX: National Educational Laboratory, 1976.

Coyle, Laurie, Gail Hershatter, and Emily Honig. "Women at Farrah: An Unfinished Story." In *Mexican Women in the United States: Struggles Past and Present,* edited by Magdalena Mora and Adelaida del Castillo. Occasional paper no. 2. Los Angeles, CA: UCLA Chicano Studies Research Center Publications, 1980.

De la Trinidad, Maritza. "Mexican Americans and the Push for Culturally Relevant Education: The Bilingual Education Movement in Tucson, 1958–1969." *History of Education* 44, no. 3 (2015): 316–38.

Delgado Bernal, Dolores. "Chicana School Resistance and Grassroots Leadership: Providing an Alternative History of the 1968 East Los Angeles Blowouts." PhD. diss., University of California, Los Angeles, 1997.

De León, Arnoldo. *Mexican Americans in Texas: A Brief History.* 2nd ed. Wheeler, IL: Harlan Davidson, 1999.

Díaz, Ella María. *Flying under the Radar with the Royal Chicano Air Force: Mapping a Chicano/a Art History.* Austin: University of Texas Press, 2017.

Dimas, Pete, ed. *Here We Stand: Chicanos Por La Causa and Arizona's Chicano/a Resurgence, 1968–1974.* Phoenix: Chicanos Por La Causa, 2019.

Echeverría, Darius V. *Aztlán Arizona: Mexican American Educational Empowerment, 1968–1978.* Tucson: University of Arizona Press, 2014.

Enríquez, Sandra Ivette. "El barrio unido jamás será vencido! Neighborhood Grassroots Activism and Community Preservation in El Paso, Texas." PhD diss., University of Houston, 2016.

Escalante, Alicia. "A Letter from the Chicana Welfare Rights Organization." *Encuentro Femenil* 1 (1973): 15–19.

Espino, Virginia. "Women Sterilized as They Give Birth: Forced Sterilization and the Chicana Resistance in the 1970s." In *Las Obreras: Chicana Politics of*

*Work and Family*, edited by Vicki L. Ruiz and Chon Noriega, 65–82. Los Angeles: UCLA Chicano Studies Research Center Publications, 2000.

Espinosa, Gastón, and Mario T. García. *Mexican American Religions: Spirituality, Activism, and Culture*. Durham, NC: Duke University Press, 2008.

Espinoza, Dionne. "'The Partido Belongs to Those Who Will Work for It': Chicana Organizing and Leadership in the Texas Raza Unida Party, 1970–1990." *Aztlán* 36, no. 1 (2011): 191–211.

———. "'Revolutionary Sisters': Women's Solidarity and Collective Identification among Chicana Brown Berets in East Los Angeles, 1967–1970." *Aztlán* 26, no. 1 (2001): 17–58.

Espinoza, Dionne, María Eugenia Cotera, and Maylei Blackwell, eds. *Chicana Movidas: New Narratives of Activism and Feminism in the Movement Era*. Austin: University of Texas Press, 2018.

Esquibel, Antonio, ed. *Message to Aztlán: Selected Writings of Rodolfo "Corky" Gonzales*. Houston, TX: Arte Público Press, 2001.

Estrada, Leobardo F., F. Chris García, Reynaldo Flores Macías, and Lionel Maldonado. "Chicanos in the United States: History of Exploitation and Resistance." *Daedalus* 110, no. 2 (1981): 101–31.

Fanon, Franz. *The Wretched of the Earth*. New York: Grove Press, 2005.

Ferris, Susan, and Ricardo Sandoval. *The Fight in the Fields: César Chávez and the Farmworkers Movement*. New York: Harcourt Brace, 1997.

Fisch, Louise Ann. *All Rise: Reynaldo G. Garza, The First Mexican American Federal Judge*. College Station: Texas A&M University Press, 1996.

Flores, Estevan T. "The Mexican-Origin People in the United States and Marxist Thought in Chicano Studies." In *The Left Academy: Marxist Scholarship on American Campuses*, edited by Bertell Ollman and Edward Vernoff, 3:103–38. New York: Praeger, 1986.

Flores, Kathy. "Chicano Attitudes toward Birth Control." *Imágenes de la Chicana* 1: 19–21 (1974).

Gambone, James V. "Bilingual Bicultural Educational Civil Rights: The May 25th Memorandum and Oppressive School Practices." PhD diss., University of New Mexico, 1973.

García, Alma M., ed. *Chicana Feminist Thought: The Basic Historical Writings*. New York: Routledge, 1997.

García, Ignacio M. *Chicanismo: The Forging of a Militant Ethos among Mexican Americans*. Tucson: University of Arizona Press, 1997.

———. *Hector P. García: In Relentless Pursuit of Justice*. Houston, TX: Arte Público Press, 2002.

———. *United We Win: The Rise and Fall of La Raza Unida*. Tucson: University of Arizona Press, 1989.

———. *Viva Kennedy!* College Station: Texas A&M University Press, 2000.

García, Mario T. *Católicos: Resistance and Affirmation in Chicano Catholic History*. Austin: University of Texas Press, 2008.

———. *Chicano Liberation Theology: The Writings and Documents of Richard Cruz and Católicos por La Raza*. Dubuque, IA: Kendall Hunt, 2009.

———. *The Chicano Movement: Perspectives from the Twenty-First Century*. New York: Routledge, 2014.

———. *A Dolores Huerta Reader*. Albuquerque: University of New Mexico Press, 2008.

———, ed. *The Gospel of César Chávez: My Faith in Action*. Lanham, MD: Sheed & Ward, 2007.

———. *The Making of a Mexican American Mayor: Raymond L. Telles of El Paso*. Tucson: University of Arizona Press, 2018.

———. *Memories of Chicano History: The Life and Narrative of Bert Corona*. Berkeley: University of California Press, 1994.

———. *Mexican Americans: Leadership, Ideology, and Identity, 1930–1960*. New Haven, CT: Yale University Press, 1989.

García, Mario T., and Sal Castro. *Blowout: Sal Castro and the Chicano Struggle for Educational Justice*. Chapel Hill: University of North Carolina Press, 2011.

García, Matt. *From the Jaws of Victory: The Triumph and Tragedy of César Chávez and the Farm Worker Movement*. Los Angeles: University of California Press, 2012.

García, Richard A. "The Chicano Movement and the Mexican American Community." *Socialist Review* 8, nos. 40–41 (1978): 72–78.

Gerry, Martin H. "Cultural Myopia: The Need for a Corrective Lens." *Journal of School Psychology* 11, no. 4 (1973): 307–15.

Gómez-Quiñones, Juan. "The First Steps: Chicano Labor Conflict and Organizing, 1900–1920." *Aztlan* 3 (Spring 1972): 13–50.

———. *Mexican Students por La Raza: The Chicano Student Movement in Southern California, 1967–1977*. Santa Barbara, CA: Editorial La Causa, 1978.

———. *Sembradores: Ricardo Flores Magón y el Partido Liberal Mexicano*. Los Angeles: UCLA Chicano Studies Research Center Publications, 1973.

Gonzales, Rodolfo "Corky." "Chicano Nationalism: The Key to Unity for La Raza." *The Militant*, March 30, 1970. Reprinted in *A Documentary History of the Mexican Americans*, edited by Wayne Moquin and Charles Van Doren, 488–93. New York: Bantam Books, 1971.

———. *I Am Joaquín/Yo Soy Joaquín*. New York: Bantam Books, 1972.

———. "We Demand: Statement of Chicanos in the Southwest on the Poor People's Campaign." In *Aztlán: An Anthology of Mexican American Literature*, edited by Luis Valdez and Stan Steiner, 218–21. New York: Vintage Books, 1972.

González, Gilbert G. *Chicano Education in the Era of Segregation*. Philadelphia: Balch Institute Press, 1990.

González-Berry, Erlinda. "Which Language Will Our Children Speak? The Span-
    ish Language and Public Education Policy in New Mexico, 1890–1930." In
    *The Contested Homeland: A Chicano History of New Mexico*, edited by
    Erlinda González-Berry and David R. Maciel, 169–90. Albuquerque: Univer-
    sity of New Mexico Press, 2000.
Griswold del Castillo, Richard, and Arnoldo De León, *North to Aztlán: A History
    of Mexican Americans in the United States*. New York: Twayne, 1996.
Griswold del Castillo, Richard, and Richard García. *César Chávez: A Triumph of
    Spirit*. Norman: University of Oklahoma Press, 1995.
Guajardo, Miguel A., and Francisco J. Guajardo. "The Impact of Brown on the
    Brown of South Texas: A Micropolitical Perspective on the Education of
    Mexican Americans in a South Texas Community." *American Educational
    Research Journal* 41, no. 3 (2004): 501–26.
Gutiérrez, David G. *Walls and Mirrors: Mexican Americans, Mexican Immi-
    grants, and the Politics of Ethnicity*. Berkeley: University of California Press,
    1995.
Gutiérrez, Henry Joseph. "The Chicano Education Rights Movement and School
    Desegregation: Los Angeles, 1962–1970." PhD diss., University of California,
    Irvine, 1990.
Gutiérrez, José Ángel. *The Eagle Has Eyes: The FBI Surveillance of César Estrada
    Chávez of the United Farmworkers Union of America, 1965–1975*. East Lan-
    sing: Michigan State University Press, 2019.
———. *The Making of a Chicano Militant: Lessons from Cristal*. Madison: Univer-
    sity of Wisconsin Press, 1998.
———. *Tracking King Tiger: Reies López Tijerina and the FBI*. East Lansing:
    Michigan State University Press, 2019.
Haney-López, Ian F. *White by Law: The Legal Construction of Race*. New York:
    New York University Press, 1996.
Hernández, José Amaro. *Mutual Aid for Survival: The Case of the Mexican Amer-
    ican*. Malabar, FL: Robert E. Krieger, 1983.
Hernández, Patricia. "Lives of Chicana Activists: The Chicano Student Movement
    (A Case Study)." In *Mexican Women in the United States: Struggles Past and
    Present*, edited by Magdalena Mora and Adelaida R. del Castillo, 7–16.
    Los Angeles: UCLA Chicano Studies Research Center Publications, 1980.
Hinojosa, Felipe. *Latino Mennonites: Civil Rights, Faith, and Evangelical Cul-
    ture*. Baltimore: Johns Hopkins University Press, 2014.
*The Invisible Minority*. Report of the NEA-Tucson Survey on the Teaching of
    Spanish to the Spanish-Speaking. Washington, DC: Department of Rural
    Education/National Education Association, 1966.
Johnson, Benjamin Heber. *Revolution in Texas: How a Forgotten Rebellion and
    Its Bloody Suppression Turned Mexicans into Americans*. New Haven, CT:
    Yale University Press, 2005.

Kaplowitz, Craig A. *LULAC, Mexican Americans, and National Policy.* College Station: Texas A&M University Press, 2005.

Laney, Garrine P. *The Voting Rights Act of 1965, As Amended: Its History and Current Issues.* Hauppauge, NY: Nova Science, 2008.

"Las Gorras Blancas." In *Testimonio: A Documentary History of the Mexican American Struggle for Civil Rights,* edited by F. Arturo Rosales, 29–30. Houston: Arte Público Press, 2000.

Macías, Ysidro Ramón. "The Chicano Movement." *Wilson Library Bulletin,* March 1970. Reprinted in *A Documentary History of the Mexican Americans,* edited by Wayne Moquin and Charles Van Doren, 499–506. New York: Bantam Books, 1971.

Madrid, Josie, Chata Mercado, Priscilla Pardo, and Anita Ramírez. "Chicanas in Prison." *Regeneración* 2 (1973): 53–54.

Mares, Renne. "La Pinta: The Myth of Rehabilitation." *Encuentro Femenil* 1 (1974): 27–29.

Mariscal, George. *Aztlán and Viet Nam: Chicano and Chicana Experiences of the War.* Berkeley: University of California Press, 1999.

———. *Brown-Eyed Children of the Sun: Lessons from the Chicano Movement, 1965–1975.* Albuquerque: University of New Mexico Press, 2005.

Márquez, Benjamin. *Constructing Identities in Mexican American Political Organizations.* Austin: University of Texas Press, 2003.

———. *LULAC: The Evolution of a Mexican American Political Organization.* Austin: University of Texas Press, 1993.

Martínez, Clemencia. "Welfare Families Face Forced Labor." *La Raza* 1 (January 1972): 41.

Martínez, Elizabeth Sutherland, and Enriqueta Longeaux y Vásquez. *Viva La Raza! The Struggle of the Mexican-American People.* New York: Doubleday, 1974.

Martínez, George A. "The Legal Construction of Race: Mexican Americans and Whiteness." *Harvard Latino Law Review* 2 (1997): 321–47.

Martínez, Richard Edward. *PADRES: The National Chicano Priest Movement.* Austin: University of Texas Press, 2005.

McCarthy, Jim, with Ron Sansoe. *Voices of Latin Rock: The People and Events That Created This Sound.* Milwaukee, WI: Hal Leonard, 2004.

Medina, Lara. *Las Hermanas: Chicana/Latina Religious-Political Activism in the U.S. Catholic Church.* Philadelphia: Temple University Press, 2005.

Meier, Matt S., and Feliciano Ribera. *The Chicanos: A History of Mexican Americans.* New York: Hill and Wang, 1972.

———. *Mexican Americans/American Mexicans: From Conquistadors to Chicanos.* San Francisco, CA: Hill and Wang, 1994.

Memmi, Albert. *The Colonizer and the Colonized.* Boston: Beacon Press, 1991.

Montejano, David. *Anglos and Mexicans in the Making of Texas, 1836–1986*. Austin: University of Texas Press, 1987.

———. *Quixote's Soldiers: A Local History of the Chicano Movement, 1966–1981*. Austin: University of Texas Press, 2010.

Morales, Armando. *Ando sangrando*. Los Angeles, CA: Perspectiva Publications, 1972.

Morin, Raul. *Among the Valiant: Mexican Americans in WW II and Korea*. Los Angeles, CA: Borden, 1963.

Muñoz, Carlos, Jr. "The Politics of Protest and Chicano Liberation: A Case Study of Repression and Cooperation." *Aztlan* 5, nos. 1–2 (1974): 119–41.

———. *Youth, Identity, Power*. New York: Verso, 1990.

National Association of Latino Elected and Appointed Officials (NALEO). *A Profile of Latino Elected Officials in the United States and Their Progress since 1996*. Los Angeles, CA: NALEO Education Fund, 2007.

Navarro, Armando. *The Cristal Experiment: A Chicano Struggle for Community Control*. Madison: University of Wisconsin Press, 1998.

———. "The Evolution of Chicano Politics." *Aztlan* 5, nos. 1–2 (1974): 57–84.

———. *Mexican American Youth Organization: Avant-Garde of the Chicano Movement*. Austin: University of Texas Press, 1995.

NietoGomez, Anna. "The Chicana–Perspectives for Education." In *Chicana Feminist Thought: The Basic Historical Writings*, edited by Alma M. García, 130–31. New York: Routledge, 1997.

———. "Francisca Flores, the League of Mexican American Women, and the Comisión Femenil Mexicana Nacional, 1958–1975." In *Chicana Movidas: New Narratives of Activism and Feminism in the Movement Era*, edited by Dionne Espinoza, María Eugenia Cotera, and Maylei Blackwell, 33–50. Austin: University of Texas Press, 2018.

———. "Madres por la justicia." *Encuentro Femenil* 1 (Spring 1973): 12–19.

Ogletree, Earl J., and David Garcia, eds. *Education of the Spanish-Speaking Urban Child*. Springfield, IL: Charles C. Thomas, 1975.

Ontiveros, Randy. *In the Spirit of a New People: The Cultural Politics of the Chicano Movement*. New York: New York University Press, 2013.

Oropeza, Lorena. *The King of Adobe: Reies López Tijerina, Lost Prophet of the Chicano Movement*. Chapel Hill: University of North Carolina Press, 2019.

———. *Raza Sí! Guerra No! Chicano Protest and Patriotism during the Viet Nam War Era*. Berkeley: University of California Press, 2005.

Oropeza, Lorena, and Dionne Espinoza, eds. *Enriqueta Vásquez and the Chicano Movement: Writings from El Grito del Norte*. Houston, TX: Arte Público Press, 2006.

Orozco, Cynthia E. *No Mexicans, Women, or Dogs Allowed: The Rise of the Mexican American Civil Rights Movement*. Austin: University of Texas Press, 2010.

————. "Sexism in Chicano Studies and in the Community." In *Chicana Voices: Intersections of Class, Race, and Gender*, edited by Teresa Cordova, Norma Cantu, Gilberto Cardenas, Juan Garcia, and Christine M. Sierra, 11–18. Albuquerque: University of New Mexico Press, 1993.

Padilla, Beverly. "Chicanas and Abortion." In *Chicana Feminist Thought: The Basic Historical Writings*, edited by Alma M. García, 120–22. New York: Routledge, 1997.

Pagán, Eduardo Obregón. *Murder at the Sleepy Lagoon: Zoot Suits, Race, and Riot in Wartime L.A.* Durham: University of North Carolina Press, 2003.

Parachini, Lawrence F. *A Political History of the Special Impact Program.* Cambridge, MA: Center for Community Economic Development, 1980.

Pardo, Mary. "Mexican American Women Grassroots Community Activists: Mothers of East Los Angeles." *Frontiers* 12, no. 1 (1990): 1–7.

Paredes, Américo. *With His Pistol in His Hand: A Border Ballad and Its Hero.* Austin: University of Texas Press, 1958.

Patino, Jimmy. *Raza Si, Migra No: Chicano Movement Struggles for Immigrant Rights in San Diego.* Durham: University of North Carolina Press, 2018.

Pawel, Miriam. *The Union of Their Dreams: Power, Hope, and Struggle in César Chávez's Farm Worker Movement.* New York: Bloomsbury Press, 2009.

Perales, Nina, Luis Figueroa, and Criselda G. Rivas. "Voting Rights in Texas: 1982–2006." *Review of Law and Social Justice* 17, no. 2 (2008): 713–59.

Pitti, Stephen J. *The Devil in Silicon Valley: Northern California, Race, and Mexican Americans.* Princeton, NJ: Princeton University Press, 2003.

Puckett, Myron Leslie. "Protest Politics in Education: A Case Study in the Los Angeles City School System." PhD diss., Claremont Graduate School and University Center, 1971.

Pycior, Julie Leininger. "Henry B. González." In *Profiles in Power: Twentieth-Century Texans in Washington*, edited by Kenneth E. Hendrickson, Michael L. Collins, and Patrick Cox, 294–308. Austin: University of Texas Press, 1993.

————. *LBJ & Mexican Americans: The Paradox of Power.* Austin: University of Texas Press, 1997.

Quiroz, Anthony. *Claiming Citizenship: Mexican Americans in Victoria, Texas.* College Station: Texas A&M University Press, 2005.

————. *Leaders of the Mexican American Generation: Biographical Essays.* Boulder: University Press of Colorado, 2015.

Quiroz González, Elizabeth. "The Education and Public Career of Maria L. Urquides: A Case Study of a Mexican American Community Leader." EdD diss., University of Arizona, 1986.

Ramírez, Henry M. *A Chicano in the White House: The Nixon No One Knew.* Whittier, CA: Self-published, 2013.

Ramos, Henry A. J. *The American G.I. Forum: In Pursuit of the Dream, 1948–1983.* Houston, TX: Arte Público Press, 1998.

Rendón, Armando. "La Raza—Today Not Manana." *Civil Rights Digest* (Spring 1968). Reprinted in *Mexican-Americans in the United States: A Reader*, edited by John H. Burma, 307–26. Cambridge, MA: Schenkman, 1970.

Reyes, David, and Tom Waldman. *Land of a Thousand Dances: Chicano Rock 'n' Roll from Southern California*. Albuquerque: University of New Mexico Press, 1998.

Rhinehart, Marilyn D., and Thomas H. Kreneck. "The Minimum Wage March of 1966: A Case Study in Mexican-American Politics, Labor, and Identity," *Houston Review* 11, no. 1 (1989): 27–44.

Rodríguez, Armando M. *From the Barrio to Washington: An Educator's Journey*. Albuquerque: University of New Mexico Press, 2007.

———. "Speak up Chicano," *American Education* (May 1968): 7–9. Reprinted in *Mexican-Americans in the United States: A Reader*, edited by John H. Burma, 135–40. Cambridge, MA: Schenkman, 1970.

Rodríguez, Joseph A., and Vicki L. Ruiz. "At Loose Ends: Twentieth-Century Latinos in Current United States History Textbooks." *Journal of American History* 86, no. 4 (2000): 1689–99.

Rodríguez, Marc Simon. *Rethinking the Chicano Movement*. New York: Routledge, 2015.

Rogers, Mary Beth. *Cold Anger: A Story of Faith and Power Politics*. Denton: University of North Texas Press, 2012.

Romero, Augustine F. "At War with the State in Order to Save the Lives of Our Children: The Battle to Save Ethnic Studies in Arizona." *Black Scholar* 40, no. 4 (2010): 7–15.

Romero, Yolanda G. "Adelante compañeros: The Sanitation Workers' Struggle in Lubbock, Texas, 1968–1972." In *Texas Labor History*, edited by Bruce A. Glasrud and James C. Maroney, 399–404. College Station: Texas A&M University Press, 2013.

Rosales, F. Arturo. *Chicano! The History of the Mexican American Civil Rights Movement*. 2nd ed. Houston: Arte Público Press, 1997.

———. "Chicanos Por La Causa (CPLC)." In *Latinas in the United States: A Historical Encyclopedia*, edited by Vicki L. Ruiz and Virginia Sánchez Korrol, 155. Bloomington: Indiana University Press, 2006.

———. *¡Pobre Raza! Violence, Justice, and Mobilization among México Lindo Immigrants, 1900–1936*. Austin: University of Texas Press, 1999.

Rose, Margaret. "Traditional and Nontraditional Patterns of Female Activism in the United Farm Workers of America, 1962–1980." *Frontiers* 11, no. 1 (1990): 26–32.

Rosenbaum, Robert J. *Mexicano Resistance in the Southwest*. Dallas, TX: Southern Methodist University Press, 2018.

Ruiz, Vicki L. *From Out of the Shadows*. New York: Oxford University Press, 1998.

Sánchez, George J. *Becoming Mexican American: Ethnicity, Culture, and Identity in Chicano Los Angeles, 1900–1945*. New York: Oxford University Press, 1995.

Sánchez, Gilbert. "An Analysis of the Bilingual Education Act, 1967–1968." PhD. diss., University of Massachusetts, 1973.

Sánchez, Juan O. "Encina: The Uvalde School Walkout." Master's thesis, Sul Ross State University, 1992.

———. "Walkout Cabrones: The Uvalde School Walkout of 1970." *West Texas Historical Association Year Book* 68 (1992): 122–33.

Sandoval, Alicia. "Chicana Liberation." In *Chicana Feminist Thought: The Basic Historical Writings*, edited by Alma M. García, 204–5. New York: Routledge, 1997.

Sandoval, Moises. *On the Move: A History of the Hispanic Church in the United States*. Maryknoll, NY: Orbis Books, 1990.

San Miguel, Guadalupe, Jr. *Brown, Not White: School Integration and the Chicano Movement*. College Station: Texas A&M University Press, 2001.

———. *Chicana/o Struggles for Education: Activism in the Community*. College Station: Texas A&M University Press, 2013.

———. "The Community Is Beginning to Rumble: The Origins of Chicano Educational Protest in Houston, 1965–1970." *Houston Review* 13, no. 3 (1991): 127–48.

———. *Contested Policy: The Rise and Fall of Federal Bilingual Education in the United States, 1960–2001*. Denton: University of North Texas Press, 2004.

———. *Let All of Them Take Heed: Mexican Americans and the Quest for Educational Equality in Texas, 1910–1981*. College Station: Texas A&M University Press, 2002.

———. *Tejano Proud: Tex-Mex Music in the Twentieth Century*. College Station: Texas A&M University Press, 2002.

Sepúlveda, Juan. *The Life and Times of Willie Velásquez: Su voto es su voz*. Houston, TX: Arte Público Press, 2003.

Shaw, Randy. *Beyond the Fields: César Chávez, the UFW, and the Struggle for Justice in the 21st Century*. Berkeley: University of California Press, 2008.

Shockley, John. *Chicano Revolt in a Texas Town*. Notre Dame, IN: University of Notre Dame Press, 1974.

Sioux Johnson, Henry, and William J. Hernández-M. *Educating the Mexican Americans*. Valley Forge, PA: Judson Press, 1970.

Sracic, Paul A. *San Antonio v. Rodríguez and the Pursuit of Equal Education*. Lawrence: University Press of Kansas, 2006.

Tijerina, Reies López. *They Called Me "King Tiger": My Struggle for the Land and Our Rights*. Houston: Arte Publico Press, 2000.

Torres Sánchez, Carmen María. "An Historical Inquiry into the Role of Community Activist Organizations in Dealing with the Problem of Overcrowded Elementary Schools in the Hispanic Community of Chicago, 1970–1990." EdD.
diss., Northern Illinois University, 1993.

Treviño, Jesús Salvador. *Eyewitness: A Filmmaker's Memoir of the Chicano Movement.* Houston, TX: Arte Público Press, 2001.

Trujillo, Armando. *Chicano Empowerment and Bilingual Education: Movimiento
Politics in Crystal City, Texas.* New York: Garland, 1998.

Tullos, Mary, and Dolores Hernández. "Talmadge Amendment: Welfare Continues to Exploit the Poor." *La Raza* 1 (January 1972): 10–11.

Valdez, Armando, Albert Camarillo, and Tomás Almaguer, eds. *The State of Chi-
cano Research in Family, Labor, and Migration Studies: Proceedings of the
First Stanford Symposium on Chicano Research and Public Policy.* Stanford,
CA: Stanford Research Center, 1983.

Valdez, Luis, and Stan Steiner, eds. *Aztlan: An Anthology of Mexican American
Literature.* New York: Vintage Books, 1972.

Valencia, Richard R. *Chicano Students and the Courts: The Mexican-American
Legal Struggle for Educational Equality.* New York: New York University
Press, 2008.

Vega, José E. *Education, Politics, and Bilingualism in Texas.* Washington, DC:
University Press of America, 1983.

Vigil, Ernesto B. *The Crusade for Justice: Chicano Militancy and the Government's War on Dissent.* Madison: University of Wisconsin Press, 1999.

Watson, Dwight. "The Storm Clouds of Change: The Death of José Campos Torres
and the Emergence of Triracial Politics in Houston, 1978–1980." In *Race and
the Houston Police Department, 1930–1990: A Change Did Come,* 110–29.
College Station: Texas A&M University Press, 2005.

Zamora, Emilio. *The World of the Mexican Worker in Texas.* College Station:
Texas A&M University Press, 1993.

# Index

Acuña, Rodolfo F., 78
Adelita, 137n68
Advisory Committee on Community
  Relations Service, 120n37
Advisory Committee on Mexican
  American Affairs, 75
AFL. *See* American Federation of
  Labor
AGIF. *See* American G.I. Forum
Agricultural Workers Organizing
  Committee, 33
Albuquerque, N.Mex., 13, 24, 38,
  121n45
Alianza, La, 38–39, 41, 43, 128n42
Alianza Federal de las Mercedes, 38
Alianza of Pueblos and
  Pobladores, 38
Alinsky, Saul, 85
Alonso, Braulio, 98
Amalgamated Clothing Workers of
  America, 56
American Federation of Labor (AFL),
  9, 29, 126n11
American G.I. Forum (AGIF): and
  Cabinet Committee Hearings,
  15–17, 19, 121n44; and EEOC,
  13–16; and employment,
  81–82, 109; and government
  representation, 7–8, 10, 75,
  119n29, 120n37, 139n3; and
  legislation, 11–12; and prejudice
  and stereotypes, 78, 87, 112;
  and radical movement, 1; and
  women, 42

American Smelting and Refining
  Company, 29–30
Anguiano, Guadalupe "Lupe," 22, 25,
  75, 97–98, 123n66, 123n68
ANMA. *See* Asociación Nacional
  México-Americana
anticolonialism, 48–49, 54
Aragón, Juan, 94, 147n25, 148n30
Arciniega, Tomás, 147n25
Arizona Civil Rights Commission, 57
Arizona State University (ASU),
  56–57
Arvisu, Ersi, 139n81
Asociación Nacional México-
  Americana (ANMA), 28, 30–31,
  42, 116n9, 126n16
August 29th Movement (ATM),
  53–54
Austin, Texas, 98, 127n23, 133n30
Avila, Edward de, 146n12
Ávila, Joaquín G., 73, 140n10
Azteca (band), 68
Aztecs, 49, 51
Aztlán, 48–54

Baca, Herman, 59
Badillo, Herman, 74
Baeza, André, 139n81
Bañuelos, Romana Acosta, 77
Becker, Charles, 86
Beeville, Texas, 95
Bell Laundry, 57
Benavides, Albert, 86
Benites, Joseph R., 82

167

civil rights movement, 3, 5–6, 31–32,
41, 43, 48, 108
Civil Service Commission, 142n25
Cold War, 2, 30–31
Coleman Report, 123n64
colleges: access to, 91, 145n7;
and Chicana students, 62,
67; and curriculum, 61; and
discrimination, 57; and El
Plan de Santa Barbara, 50–51;
and scholarships, 143n45; and
student activists, 1, 16–18,
32–33, 43–44, 56, 62, 84–85
colonialism, 48, 54
Columbia University, 73
Comisión Femenil Mexicana
Nacional, 129n56
Committee on Chicano Rights (CCR),
58–59
Committee on New Frontier Policy in
the Americas, 7
Committee on Opportunities for
Spanish-Speaking Affairs
(COSSA), 76–77, 120n39,
123n62, 142n25
Communist Party, 30, 53, 126n16
Communities Organized for Public
Service (COPS), 84–86, 144n59
community development corporations
(CDCs), 81–84
Community Service Organization
(CSO), 8, 32, 42, 85, 119n29,
126n18, 139n1
Compeán, Mario, 84
Compton, Calif., 73
Conde, Carlos, 77
Congressional Hispanic Caucus,
70, 74
Congress of Industrial Organizations
(CIO), 29–30, 126n11
Congress of Spanish-Speaking
Peoples, 28

Connally, John, 9, 15, 18, 119n26
Coors Brewing Company, 81
COPS. *See* Communities Organized
for Public Service
Corona, Bert, 1, 14, 17, 58–59
Corpus Christi, Texas, 82, 99, 109
Corrada del Río, Baltasar, 74
Cortés, Ernesto, Jr., 84–85, 144n54
Cortez, Gregorio, 28
Cortina, Juan, 27
COSSA. *See* Committee on
Opportunities for Spanish-
Speaking Affairs
Cota, Rosita, 97, 100
CPLC. *See* Chicanos por La Causa
Crowther, Jack P., 123n70
Crusade for Justice, 16, 40–41, 43,
47, 49
Crystal City, Texas, 9–10, 45–46, 60

Dana, Bill, 78–79, 142n32
Daniel, Price, 9
Dawson, N.Mex., 32
De Baca, Fernando, 77
de la Garza, Eligio "Kika," 74,
150n45
Delano, Calif., 32–34, 36–37
del Castillo, Adelaida R., 136n62
Del Rio, Texas, 95, 109, 111
De Luna, John, 139n81
Democratic Party, 7–10, 40, 42,
118n10, 129n51
Democratic Women Committee,
129n51
Dent, Teresa, 93
Denver, Colo., 24, 40, 45, 47, 49,
52–54, 83, 92, 132n25
Denver Community Development
Corporation, 83
Department of Defense, U.S., 14
Department of Education, U.S. 20,
22, 90, 98–99

CPSIA information can be obtained
at www.ICGtesting.com
Printed in the USA
LVHW091544030222
709936LV00010BA/1299